THE PACKER'S FIELD MANUAL

FEATURING
THE DECKER PACK SADDLE

By Bob Hoverson

PHOTOGRAPHY & ILLUSTRATIONS BY ROGER INGHRAM

THE PACKER'S FIELD MANUAL

Featuring The Decker Pack Saddle

By BOB HOVERSON

Photography and Illustrations by Roger Inghram

Copyright 2005 by Bob Hoverson

Published in the United States of America

Second Printing, June 2009

ISBN 1-931291-42-X

Library of Congress Control Number 2004118147

STONEYDALE PRESS PUBLISHING COMPANY
523 Main Street • P.O. Box 188
Stevensville, Montana 59870
Phone: 406-777-2729
Webnsite: www.stoneydale.com

TABLE OF CONTENTS

Cover Photo: This scene shows the U.S.D.A. Forest Service's Northern Region Pack Train crossing the North Fork of the Sun River near Gates Park in Montana's Bob Marshall Wilderness. Photo courtesy Forest Service.

PREFACE

The purpose of this packing field manual is to provide "state-of-the-art" basic instruction in the art of mule and horse packing. It is presented in a "field manual" size book so it may be carried in a saddle bag or other convenient location to be readily available for easy reference. Although this manual emphasizes the **Decker Style** of packing, much of the information presented will apply to any packing technique.

This is not a "story book" but rather a source for specific information on equipment and techniques required for efficient mule and horse packing utilizing the Decker Packing Style. Special emphasis is given to **Safety** and **Leave No Trace / Leave Only Tracks** practices.

I was drawn into the world of packing years ago because I have always been an avid elk hunter. One of my greatest pleasures in life is to assemble a hunting camp – tents, stoves, lanterns, cots, sleeping bags, tables, chairs, groceries, etc. – cargo it all up and pack it into a remote hunting camp for extended periods of time. I have adopted a philosophy of optimizing loads and minimizing the number of stock, while still having the most comfortable and environmentally compatible camp as possible.

I have been fortunate in my life to have rubbed elbows with some of the very best packers, outfitters, and stock handlers in the country. In this manual I will pass on to you numerous techniques and practices for safe and efficient mule and horse packing that I have acquired over more than twenty-five years of packing and camping in the back country of Montana and Idaho.

ACKNOWLEDGMENTS

I want to thank all those who have contributed information, pictures, time, equipment, knowledge and general support to the preparation of this manual. Individuals who have had direct involvement in the writing of this manual are:

•Roger Inghram – I can't thank Roger enough for his photography and art work, not to mention the days (weeks) spent filming, editing, drafting, and traveling. This book would not have been written without Roger's help!

•Wendy Sandefur – My daughter Wendy was my rough draft editor through this whole process. Proper sentence structure is not my long suit, she about wore out her red pencil correcting my English.

•Smoke Elser – Although Smoke was not "directly involved", everything I know about Decker Style Packing initially came from Smoke. I first met Smoke and attended his packing clinic in 1980. Smoke's understanding of packing philosophy and his ability to teach it are second to none. I have had the privilege of working with Smoke in many of his clinics over the years. He is truly the "Guru" of Decker Packing.

•Mark Pengelly & Doug Hunt – Mark and Doug are colleagues who I work with everyday. They provided the technical review of this manual, and they were my all-around "sounding board" during the writing phase. Over the years we've ridden thousands of trail miles together and moved a million pounds (literally) of freight. These guys are Packers!

• A special thanks goes to my good friend Dale Burk of Stoneydale Press Publishing Company, who I first met and hunted elk with some thirty-five years ago. Dale asked me to write this book and I would never have started this project without his encouragement and support.

Others who have contributed to this effort:
•Russ Barnett, Outfitter Supply, Columbia Falls, Montana – Photograph
•Tim Mueller – Model and book review
•Frank Bonde – Model and filming venue
•Tim Resch – Model and photograph
•Greg Cover – Photographs
•Ally Sandefur – (my granddaughter) Model
•Jennifer Botkin – (my daughter) Typing

Finally, I must thank my entire family for putting up with me (or should I say without me) the past few months as I hid away and worked on this book. Again, thanks to all of the above for assisting me in this endeavor!

DEDICATION

This effort is dedicated to my family. To my daughters, Wendy and Jennifer; son-in-laws, Rick Sandefur and Bob Botkin; and to my grandchildren, Shelby and Ally (Wendy & Rick) and Adam and Kayla (Jen & Bob). They are my reason for being and provide an ever increasing "return on my investment".

Most of all I dedicate this book to my wife Nan. We started first grade together at the age of six and have been married for 37 years at this writing. I have had a wonderful and rewarding life, and it is obvious it would not have been the same without Nan. Our beautiful family and my career are a direct result of her gentle (and not so gentle) coaxing, pushing, and prodding.

I love you all!

Decker pack saddles are durable, humane, and versatile.

INTRODUCTION

To begin let's discuss what this manual is <u>not</u>. This is not a manual on basic horsemanship and riding. It is not a first aid course. It is not a cookbook. Likewise, this is not a horse/mule training manual, nor is it a survival manual. This manual is very specific to the equipment, techniques, and practices necessary to master the "art" of packing the **Decker Pack Saddle.** Supporting information relating to safety and leave-only-tracks camping practices is included, but the primary purpose of this manual is to provide a complete and handy reference for mastering the **Decker Packing Style.**

Many excellent books on packing and back country travel already exist. The "bible" I have learned from and live by is **Packin' In On Mules and Horses** by Smoke Elser and Bill Brown. Other excellent sources of packing information are: ***Horses Hitches and Rocky Trails*** by Joe Back, ***Manual of Pack Transportation*** by H.W. Daly, ***Horse Packing in Pictures*** by Francis W. Davis, Oliver C. Hill's **Packing and Outfitting Field Manual,** and Stacey Gebhard's ***When Mules Wore Diamonds.*** These sources will always provide good information on packing, although some refer mainly to "Sawbuck" style packing and some have become dated and may even be out of print. Others are printed in the standard 8½ by 11-inch format which is a bit less convenient to pack around than this manual.

In any given packing situation there are numerous ways to tie on cargo that will work and get the job done. Likewise, there are many personal preferences when it comes to types of stock, saddle styles, size and material for manties, rope types and lengths, methods of putting ropes up, knots, cargoing and loading methods and techniques, etc. Regardless of the choices made, the key ingredients should always be

safety and **efficiency** for both pack animal and packer!

This manual features "The Decker Pack Saddle" and "Decker Style" of packing. Originating in the very early 1900's, Decker packing is relatively "new", as compared to Sawbuck Style Packing which has been in existence since the time of Genghis Khan. The Decker, however, has three specific qualities which makes it a superior system.

First, the Decker is a more **durable** saddle as it is constructed with steel "bows" rather than wooden crossbucks. This allows more weight on average to be carried on the saddle over a period of time, without the saddle breaking apart.

Second, the Decker is a more **humane** saddle to the pack animal. The tree can be shaped and the rigging can be adjusted to each individual animal. The Sawbuck saddle is generally a "one size fits all" situation. The Decker offers greater protection to the pack animal as it is constructed with a canvas and leather cover with wooden pack boards on each side. This cover, called a "half-breed", can be added to a Sawbuck Saddle, but original Sawbucks did not have this feature. The Decker also allows the load to be carried in a more comfortable position on the pack animal's back, rather than on the side/rib area.

The third advantage to the Decker Saddle is its **versatility**. It is relatively easy to pack large, odd shaped loads on the Decker utilizing the Decker cargoing system. The Decker easily accommodates specially constructed carriers that attach to the saddle making it very safe and efficient to pack four to twelve foot long material. Traditional Sawbuck loads are limited by the size and shape of the pannier. A heavy top load is then required, which may be difficult to balance. Adjustments in load balance can be accomplished in seconds on a Decker, whereas on a Sawbuck the load must often be completely untied and re-tied.

The Decker is, without doubt, the finest and most versatile pack saddle ever made. It can carry heavier loads with less wear and tear on the pack stock. It can be loaded and unloaded quicker than other packing styles. Greater varieties and shapes of cargo can be packed, and the load can be balanced quicker and easier than any other packing style.

So now, with our eye on safety, efficiency, and a "leave-only-tracks" philosophy, **let's go packin'.**

CHAPTER ONE

EVOLUTION OF THE DECKER PACK SADDLE

There have been many arguments as to where the Decker Pack Saddle came from and who invented it, but the version that appears to be the most plausible and factual is as follows: The first tree of its kind (with wooden bars and steel bows) was first utilized by an old-time Aparajo packer named S.C. MacDaniels in the Buffalo Hump country in central Idaho during the mining boom that occurred in that area from 1898 to 1900. Several brothers named Decker saw the practicality of the

The Aparajo saddle (circa 1900) was the predecessor to the Decker Pack Saddle.

idea, adopted it, and made some improvements to the Aparajo (pronounced ap-a-ray-ho) cover, or "half-breed" as it is known today. Although, they applied for a patent on the tree and rigging which apparently was never granted, the name "Decker Pack Saddle" stuck.

In the early 1900s the Decker Brothers established themselves as some of the finest packers in Idaho and Montana, packing thousands of pounds of equipment and supplies into the unroaded, trail-less terrain of the Selway and Lochsa Rivers, over Lolo Pass and into the Bitterroot Valley of Montana. All the while they were demonstrating the durability and versatility, as well as humane nature of the Decker saddle. Another key player in the development of the Decker saddle was a blacksmith/saddle maker named Oliver P. Robinette. Robinette is credited with developing and manufacturing hundreds of the Decker trees and pack saddles for the Decker brothers as well as for local sheepmen and other outfitters and packers of that era. The Decker Brothers could foresee a rapid increase in the use of this unique and clearly superior pack saddle and they made a deal with Robinette to market the saddle. The saddle was advertised and sold as the Decker Pack Saddle. In later years O.P. Robinette built many trees for the Forest Service. (Robinette

Trees built by Oliver P. Robinette from 1900-1945 have "OPR" inscribed on the bar.

saddle trees inscribed "OPR" on the wooden bar are considered by many to be collector's items.) Robinette built trees until his death in 1945.

The Forest Service, an agency of the United States Department of Agriculture, has played a key role in the history and development of the Decker Pack Saddle and the Decker Packing Style. Created in 1905, the Forest Service began using Decker Saddles as early as 1920. Forest officers from throughout the northwest recognized the utility of the Decker Packing Style and began to put it to use. In 1930 a "Remount Depot" was established in the Ninemile Valley west of Missoula, Montana, as a place to raise and train horses and mules, as well as train packers for the Forest Service. Horses and mules in sufficient quantity to supply fire fighters during critical fire seasons had become difficult, if not impossible, to obtain from private sources. The Decker Pack Saddle was adopted as the official saddle and packing style in Region One. Region One includes all of Montana, Northern Idaho, North Dakota, and a bit of South Dakota. Oddly enough, a line exists even today where the Sawbuck Saddle is the saddle of choice in the Southwestern states and the Decker continues to be used in the Northwest.

Part of the mission of the newly established Ninemile Remount

Ninemile Remount Depot, a USDA Forest Service facility near Huson, Montana, played a significant role in the history of the Decker Pack Saddle.

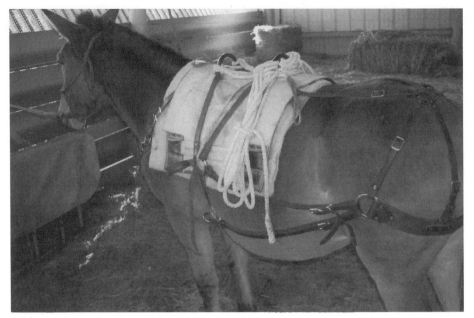

The Decker is the pack saddle of choice in Montana, northern Idaho, Washington, and Oregon.

Depot was to "develop improved methods of packing and standardize packing practices." In 1937 a standard specification for the Decker Pack Saddle was prepared, and that specification with only minor modification, is still used today as the basic design of most Decker Saddles. A copy of the 1937 Decker Saddle specification is shown on Pages 16-17.

The Ninemile Remount Depot ceased operation in 1953 and the facility became a Ranger Station on the Lolo National Forest. Closure of the Remount Depot was due largely to the fact that roads were being built to access previously unroaded and inaccessible areas. In addition, helicopters and smokejumpers had arrived on the scene to greatly assist in fire fighting efforts. It should also be noted that all throughout this time outfitters, cattlemen, sheep herders, and private individuals in the Northwest had adopted the Decker Packing Style for their own use. Stock use and packing were a "way of life" for most people in this region at that time.

A significant event that occurred in 1964 was the passage of the Wilderness Act by the United States Congress. This act set aside millions of acres nationwide that would be forever road-less. A large portion of this acreage is accessible only by foot or horse travel. In spite of the fact

The Sawback Pack Saddle is dominant in Southwestern states.

that over the past forty years we have become a "high speed-highly mechanized" society, interest in backcountry stock use today is high and continues to grow. Stock use and packing have become a very enjoyable recreational pursuit, rather than the way of life of the past.

Stock use and packing in the back country is an activity that is destined to continue for many generations. Hopefully this manual can assist "do-it-yourselfers" and professionals alike in participating in this wonderful and enjoyable activity, safely and efficiently.

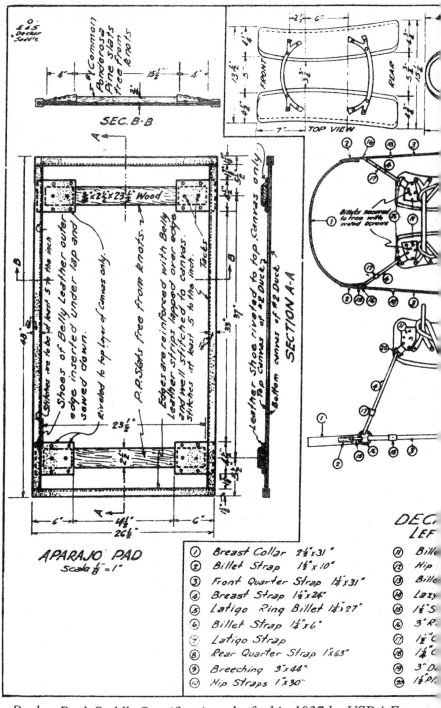

Decker Pack Saddle Specification, drafted in 1937 by USDA Forest

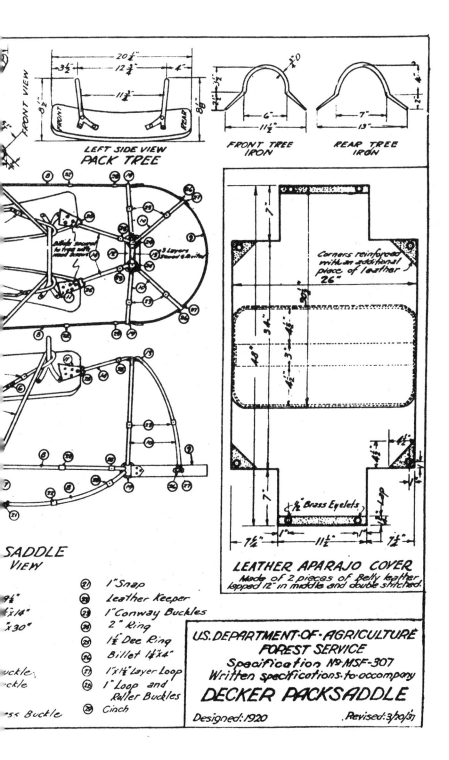

FRONT VIEW

LEFT SIDE VIEW
PACK TREE

20¼"
3½" 12¾" 4"
11¾"
8½"
8⅛"

FRONT REAR

**FRONT TREE
IRON**

2"0
¾"
4"
2⅛"
6"
11½"

**REAR TREE
IRON**

2
4"
7"
13"
2"

SADDLE
VIEW

Corners reinforced
with an additional
piece of leather
26"

30½"
34"
40"
4½"-3"-4½"

LEATHER APARAJO COVER
Made of 2 pieces of Belly leather
lapped 12" in middle and double stitched.

7"
⅜" Brass Eyelets
4½"
4½" Lap
7½" 1" 11½" 1" 7½"

㉑	1" Snap	
㉒	Leather Keeper	
㉓	1" Conway Buckles	
㉔	2" Ring	
㉕	1½" Dee Ring	
㉖	Billet 1½"x4"	
㉗	1"x1½" Layer Loop	
㉘	1" Loop and Roller Buckles	
㉙	Cinch	

9½"
½"x14"
"x30"

uckle
ckle

ss Buckle

US. DEPARTMENT OF AGRICULTURE
FOREST SERVICE
Specification No. MSF-307
Written specifications to accompany

DECKER PACKSADDLE

Designed: 1920   Revised: 3/20/37

Backcountry stock use and packing has become a very enjoyable recreational pursuit, rather than the "way of life" of the past.

CHAPTER TWO

PACK STOCK

Horses vs. Mules

The decision whether to use horses or mules, or a combination of horses and mules, for pack stock is definitely a matter of personal preference, or often times more a matter of what you have available to you. The simple fact is they all work, just some better than others.

Given a choice, I believe it is fair to say most experienced packers would prefer to pack mules and ride horses. Having said this I should point out that I personally ride a mule and pull a string of mules about a thousand miles each year. Again this is personal preference. I recognize I am trading away some advantages I might have with riding a horse, but

Both mules and horses are good pack animals, although many packers prefer mules.

I am willing to sacrifice this for the improved ride. Likewise, many packers pack horses and get along just fine. My personal preference for a pack animal, however, is definitely a mule.

Mules, in general, have certain qualities that tend to make them better overall pack animals. Mules have a much stronger **survival instinct** than do horses and they have a strong **herding instinct**. These two traits result in distinct advantages for the packer.

Given their strong survival instinct, mules very seldom do things to hurt themselves. They learn very quickly that it is easier to twist their body or walk around objects along a trail, rather than constantly bang into them. This saves wear and tear on your stock and tack, as well as whatever is in the pack. Horses often times never figure this out. If a mule becomes entangled in rope or worse yet, wire, they will often stand and wait for assistance in getting out of the predicament (or most likely they won't get into the predicament to begin with). Likewise, in a "wreck" situation while traveling down a trail (wrecks do happen, even with the best mules) once a mule realizes he is trapped, again he will usually stand or lay and wait for assistance. In similar situations, a horse often will struggle, causing even more serious injury to itself than

Mules will "bond" to a lead horse. Move the horse and generally the mules come running.

occurred from the original entanglement or wreck.

The strong herding instinct of mules can be used to a definite advantage when it comes to catching your stock or when you are in the back country and you need to contain your stock. Mules will "bond" very quickly to a horse that they have been kept with for a length of time and they will bond to a mare usually before they will bond to a gelding. Mules generally do not bond to a "lead mule" the way they will bond to a "lead horse" and although mules may buddy up in pairs or threes, generally a whole string will not bond to a lead mule. The advantage of this herding/bonding tendency is that as long as you control your horse, (not mule) you will have your mules with you. Catch the horse and the mules will want to be caught also. When in the back country, if you picket or tie your horse and turn the mules loose, your mules will wander around and graze, but they won't stray too far from your horse. Move the horse and the mules will usually come running. (Be aware, if your horse runs away, your mules will go too, and you will be walking!)

As long as I mentioned mares, I will go ahead and say I do not recommend them. If you own mares, fine, but if you have a choice, stay with geldings. You will experience fewer problems associated with kicking, biting, or general inattention to the job if you do not have mares in your string. The advantage of a "bell mare" is outweighed by the problems they can cause. A gelding will quickly be recognized as the leader and boss the same as the bell mare with far less turmoil. If you do run mares in your string, try to have several. There will be less tendency to have turmoil if several mares are present than if you just have one.

When choosing between molly (female) mules or john (male) mules, personal preference again comes into play. Some packers prefer mollies for their kinder disposition. Personally it makes no difference to me and it has been my experience the john mules have more personality, which I like. Because all mules are sterile and john mules are always gelded, the state of turmoil does not develop with mules and gelded horses as it can when a mare is present.

Mule Facts and Terminology

If you are going to become a professional or competent mule handler it is well worth your while to understand some facts and terminology about mules. Sometimes sounding good will get you as far as being good, however there is definite benefit and practical application in being familiar with the lingo. This list is not all inclusive but it will cover the necessary basics.

Mule: The sterile offspring of a male donkey and a mare horse. Mules can be trained to do anything a horse can do. In addition to being superb pack animals, they are used in harness, under saddle, and in most all equestrian sports.

Molly: A female mule.

John: A male mule. Although sterile, male mules are always gelded.

Donkey: A long-eared equine that comes in many breeds. The donkey is referred to as an ass in the Bible. Donkeys, like horses, are not sterile.

Jenny or Jennet: A female donkey.

Jack: A male donkey, usually a stallion.

Burro: Spanish for donkey, but small, usually the 9 to 12 hand size.

Hinny: The offspring of a stallion horse and a jenny ass. The hinny is a "novelty" animal and does not possess the good qualities of the mule hybrid.

Half-breed: A horse produced by breeding a purebred with a horse of different breeding. The mule could be described as a half-breed. Presumably this is why the protective cover over the Decker Saddle is called a half-breed and the lightweight cover over the half-breed is called a quarter-breed.

There are several breeds and sizes of donkeys.

A mule's mother is always a horse.

A mule is the sterile offspring of a male donkey and a mare horse.

Height of all equine is measured in "hands" or four-inch increments. This mule is 14.3 hands or 59 inches tall at the withers.

Hand: A term used in measuring height of equine. A hand equals four inches. This measurement is taken from the top of the withers in a straight line to the ground. A fifteen hand equine is 60 inches, 61 inches is expressed as 15.1 hands, 62 inches is 15.2 hands, and 63 inches is 15.3 hands. A 16 hand equine is 64 inches tall at the withers.

Mule size: A colt will generally mature taller than the mare, how much is determined by the size of the jack.

Donkey sizes: Donkeys are recognized in four sizes; Miniature which is less than 9 hands, Spanish - 9 to 12 hands, Standard – 12 to 13.2 hands, and Mammoth which is 13.2 hands and over. Good pack mules are generally bred to Standard Jacks or Mammoth Jacks. This produces pack animals big enough to carry an efficient load.

Working life: The normal working life of a mule assuming no disabling injuries is 25 to 30 years of age. In comparison, the normal working life of a horse is 20 to 25 years.

Horse and Mule Anatomy

As with mule terminology, if you want to become a competent and efficient packer there is benefit and practical application in being familiar with specific names and locations of the parts of a horse. Anatomical names are objective with no judgment of the correctness or quality of how parts fit together. In contrast, a horse or mule's "conformation" can be considered good or bad depending on the breed standards and the absence or presence of conformation defects.

Recognizing the anatomical features of a mule or horse can help us describe good and bad points of conformation, we can easily make reference to actual or potential points of injury, and we can describe how saddles and tack should fit relative to a particular animal's anatomy and conformation.

ANATOMY OF A MULE

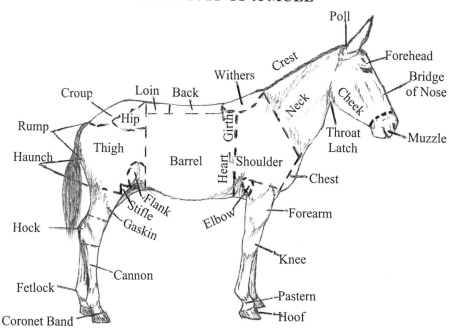

Equine Anatomy – recognizing anatomical features can help us describe how well saddles and tack fit.

—25—

Traits of a Good Pack Animal

One thing I have found over the years is that it is extremely difficult to buy horses or mules for other people. The standard order is for an animal that is sound and gentle, young, well broke, and cheap! Young and well broke most often do not go together and a broke horse or mule for one person may not be broke well enough for another. Additionally, most horses and mules are no longer cheap. Animals that cost $300 to $500 twenty-five years ago are now costing $2,000 to $2,500. In this section I will merely point out some key factors to consider when you are looking at a potential pack animal for purchase.

A few things to consider before you begin your search for a pack animal are your own personal preferences. First of all, do you want a horse or a mule? Do you need an animal that will both pack and ride, or do you strictly need a pack animal? If you are looking for a horse, will you take a mare as well as a gelding? (As mentioned earlier, I don't recommend mares, but it's definitely a conscious decision you need to make.) Are you concerned about color, and what size of an animal will meet your needs? If you are five-foot four, a sixteen hand mule is probably not a good choice for you. A good average height to start at is 15 hands with a weight of 1,000 to 1,200 pounds. You then should adjust

This mule is taller than the packer, making loading very difficult.

depending on your physical capability.

Ideally, we always look for animals that will be steady and reliable. For me, the most important trait is their disposition. I am willing to trade off perfection in conformation, size, or color for an animal with a calm disposition. Other characteristics to look for are: easy to catch; not ear shy; and no kickers, biters, or animals that paw. All animals should lead readily and stand quietly to saddle or when tied. Spoiled animals that lean on you or walk on you, and generally show no respect for you, should be avoided. This type of animal will hurt you in the long run. Another very important trait is the ability to pick up and handle their feet. Many animals are not perfect to shoe, however, they should not be a hazard or liability at shoeing time.

Age is another important consideration. If you are an experienced stock person and have the ability to train stock, buying animals at age three to five may be appropriate for you. For either horses or mules, very light packing can occur at age three, moderate at age four, and near full weight at age five. Mules and horses will continue to grow and develop to age seven so care should be taken to not overload until they are fully developed. Stock purchased in the eight to twelve age-class should be a good value for the long haul. Assuming they have been trained properly and have been used enough to gain valuable experience they will still have fifteen to twenty good years left in them.

Determining good conformation may require more experience than deciding on personal preferences. Poor conformation can lead to unsoundness. In general stock should be balanced front to back and left side to right side with no apparent abnormalities. The parts of a horse or mule should be balanced and in proportion with one another. A large head on a small bodied animal, or tiny feet on a large animal can lead to structural breakdown over time.

Always look for straight legs, see figures 2-9, a-d. A horse that does not have straight legs is more likely to put excess strain on ligaments and tendons. They may appear sound today, but a crooked leg can take years off of an animal's working life.

Good feet are essential to mountain horses and mules. Although anatomically they are the same, horse and mule feet differ in conformation. A mule's foot is generally straighter walled, harder and more durable than a horse's foot. A horse's foot is generally larger then a mule's foot and, as mentioned above, small, dainty, feet with thin soles and thin walls will generally not hold up.

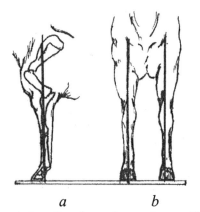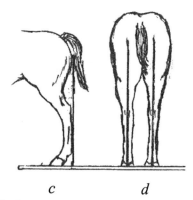

| a | b | c | d |

2-9 – Good conformation calls for straight legs.

Mules generally don't have prominent withers like a horse, but some wither is important. It is difficult to balance a saddle on a round or "mutton withered" mule.

Determining soundness for the long haul can be very difficult if not impossible. A pre-purchase exam conducted by a good equine veterinarian is an excellent tool to head off problems related to soundness. An equine veterinarian will also be able to assist you with judging all the previously mentioned traits.

CHAPTER THREE

SAFETY BASICS

Possibly the greatest need of all stock users is a set of simple instructions in safe use and care of these rather large animals. Safe use and care should not only include the individual, but the animal as well. Horses and mules are expensive, they are subject to injury, and they can be dangerous if they get into the kind of jam that requires struggling for survival. When a horse is being disorderly, is subject to pain or injury, or is going through an experience that causes him to have fear, his reactions may not be predictable. At such times, even an experienced horseman cannot always anticipate the animal's reaction or his next move. Therefore, proper care and use of the horse or mule calls for safe practices. ALWAYS!

In making suggestions for safe practices while using animals, we must consider the natural instincts and habits of the horse or mule. These natural instincts are explained in detail in Chapter Four. Remember, there is a reason for the following suggestions! Time and space do not permit a full explanation for each, but if each is practiced faithfully, some expensive and painful experiences can be prevented. Hopefully I will not be criticized by experience packers for suggestions that are not exactly as they would have them. In the horsemanship and packing business there are often several ways to accomplish the same objective, i.e., there may be ten different ways to tie a knot to restrain an animal or to hold a pack in place. However, my experience tells me that some methods are definitely safer and more efficient than others. As long as you can explain a **safe reason** for why you do what you do, then it is probably OK. To merely say "this is the way I was taught to do it" may not be sufficient. The key is to be mindful of always using safe practices! Safe practices and safe techniques must become habit. They should happen automatically. If some painful and expensive injuries can be prevented, our goal will be accomplished.

USE SAFE PRACTICES, ALWAYS!

Working Around Stock

• Always speak to an animal when approaching from any direction. Never surprise an animal. They will react and possibly injure themselves or you.

• Stand opposite the left shoulder when initiating contact with an animal. This is the safest place to stand when working around any horse or mule.

• When it is necessary to catch a horse or mule, approach from the left side and place your hand on the neck just in front of the shoulder.

• If an animal is loose and will only allow you to approach it from directly in front, place your hand upon it as far from the tip of its nose as possible. If you cannot reach its jaw or neck, rub very lightly between the eyes. The proper place to touch it is on the neck, just in

Standing in the "safe zone" at mule's left shoulder.

Passing under neck of a tied animal is very hazardous.

front of the shoulder on the left.

• If an animal is tied solidly, always stay away from a position directly in front of him. A tied horse or mule can only move in two directions, forward or backward. If it is tied solidly enough that it cannot go backward and it has any fear, of you or anything else, it is going to go forward right over the top of you.

• If you are on one side of an animal and desire to be on the other side, do not pass under his head or neck. Speak to him, place your hand on his hip and pass directly behind him to the other side. Maintain hand contact all the time. Always remember, if the animal became unruly while you were crawling under the tied lead rope, you would be in a very dangerous position. As stated before, a safe practice is to stay away from a position directly in front of a horse that is tied solidly.

Tying Stock

Anyone who uses stock **must** know how to **correctly** tie an animal.

Wrapping lead rope around your hand can result in severely pinched fingers or worse.

Many accidents, injuries, and inconveniences occur every year because of improper tying. **THERE IS NO EXCUSE FOR IMPROPER TYING!!**

√ Always tie with a quick release knot.

√ Never put your fingers through a loop.

√ Always use safe and proper equipment.

√ Tie at the proper height and length.

√ Tie to a solid object.

A quick release knot will allow you to free an animal in a safe manner if he becomes unruly. Also, an improperly tied knot can be pulled so tight that it must be cut to free it. This results in unnecessary expense, inconvenience, and sets up a possible future safety hazard due to a lead rope that is too short. A standard horse tie knot is illustrated in Chapter Nine.

Halters: Halters must be strong so they will not break under any circumstance. A weak halter is an unsafe halter!! Even so, the halter should be relatively lightweight as the animal must carry it on its head all of the time when being used. (When packing and riding in the mountains it is customary to leave the halter on under the bridle.) A halter should never be left on when the animal is turned loose in a pasture. Halters

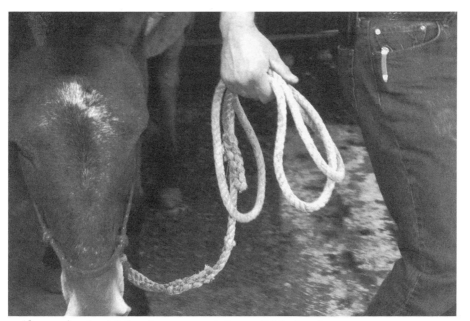
Always lead with lead rope straight or folded in loops.

should be constructed so they are relatively maintenance free and affordable. When they are properly constructed, flat nylon, good quality leather, or tightly braided climbing rope make good halters. The fewer number of snaps and buckles the better. Any rivets in a halter (leather) should be made of solid copper and never be tubular rivets.

Lead ropes: It is my opinion that the lead rope should be eye spliced on one end and attached directly to the halter. The lead should never be attached with a snap of any kind!! Snaps are a weak link that can easily break under the strain of a horse that pulls back. Any horse or mule, no matter how gentle, is capable of pulling back if startled or frightened.

The type and quality of the lead rope is just as important as the halter. I recommend a 12 foot long, ½ inch diameter, three strand composite rope (see Chapter Nine). This results in a strong, durable, and safe halter when the lead rope is eye-spliced and attached to the halter, and back-spliced on the running end to prevent fraying. Cotton ropes rot with age and they absorb water, freezing in cold weather. Polypropylene and Manila will fray and are hard on your hands. Multi-strand braided nylon is slick and does not hold a knot well. Also, it cannot be eye-spliced or back-spliced.

Never wrap or loop a lead rope around your hand. It should always be carried in folds. Lead ropes that are too small in diameter will encourage you to wrap them around your hand. Lead ropes that are too large in diameter are difficult to hang onto. Again, I recommend ½ inch diameter, three strand, composite rope.

Tying Tips

Always tie a horse or mule to a **solid** anchor at a height midway between the tip of the animal's nose and the eyes when the animal is standing at a normal rested position. If he is tied to such things as a rotten post or rotten limb, your tent frame, or your truck mirror, there is a great danger to you and the animal should stress on the lead rope cause the anchor to move or break and frighten him. Anything that can be moved is a dangerous anchor for a horse or mule. An animal should never be tied **longer** than the distance from the ground to the halter when the head is at normal height.

As mentioned previously, always tie an animal with a knot that can be easily untied, (see Chapter Nine).

When tying or leading an animal, it is always a dangerous practice to tie a rope around an animal's neck. If a rope must be tied around the

Tie at a height midway between the tip of the animal's nose and the eyes.

neck, a bowline knot should be used as it can be untied under strain (or after heavy strain), and it will not allow the rope to draw tight and choke the animal. This knot is illustrated in Chapter Nine.

It is never a good practice to tie with bridle reins. Reins are not designed to withstand the stress of a 1,000-plus-pound animal. You will only tear up equipment and maybe end up walking home to boot. Tying with reins can also result in serious injury to your horse's mouth or head. There is no replacement for a good strong halter and halter rope when tying stock.

Hauling Stock

Stock hauling is most often done with trucks or trailers specifically equipped for hauling up to ten head of horses and/or mules in a single load. In the past twenty years we have seen a rather dramatic switch from truck dominance to trailer dominance. Vehicle manufacturers have greatly improved ¾ ton and 1 ton pickups in terms of power, suspension, and people comforts making them an excellent vehicle for towing horse trailers. In addition, horse trailer manufacturers have greatly improved the quality of trailers with gooseneck styles, lighter weight aluminum, and even adding deluxe living quarters.

Regardless of the use of either stock trucks or pickup/trailer combinations, safety concerns are very similar. It is essential to check and keep in good working order at all times the hitch, floor boards, lights, tires, and brakes. For most back country type use, trailers will likely be pulled over many miles of rough gravel roads. Rattles, noise, and mechanical or structural irregularities must be located and corrected in a timely manner.

Be sure your truck has enough power and suspension to handle your trailer. Heavy duty rubber floor mats and side mats will give stock traction to stand up in the trailer and will provide protection from kicking on the walls. A round rear bumper on the trailer will greatly protect the stock's lower legs as they exit the trailer. Stock will need a space of about seven feet long by two feet wide inside the trailer. Stock should be cross tied nose to tail in a truck or slant loaded facing the same direction in a trailer. This will offset their feet and significantly reduce foot and leg injuries.

It is the responsibility of the driver to insure a smooth trip with reasonable speed from point to point.

Mounting

Mounting is somewhat of an individual thing, depending on your height, weight and athletic ability. When you prepare to mount, examine your cinch for proper tightness. Stand at the animal's left shoulder facing toward his rear, holding the reins so there is just enough slack to relieve any tension on the bit. Hold a little more slack in the right rein than in the left rein. When this is done, if the horse jumps while being mounted, a quick pull will automatically pull his head sharply to the left and may prevent him from bucking. The motion may actually assist you in getting into the saddle. With your left hand, hold the reins at the top of the horse's neck just in front of the saddle and grasp a lock of mane to use as a balance. Holding the stirrup with the right hand and twisting it to face forward, put the toe of your left foot into the stirrup and pull yourself up and into the saddle. The right hand can assist by grabbing the saddle horn and pulling.

If you cannot perform this operation without unbalancing your horse, try this alternate method. From the same position, place the left hand on the horn with a grasp on the reins. Place the left toe in the stirrup with the aid of the right hand as before, then while jumping up and inward, grasp

Tapaderos on your riding saddle will prevent your feet from going through the stirrup.

the far side of the saddle (either the pommel or cantle, whichever works best for you), and with the right hand pull yourself into the saddle.

To dismount, pick a **safe** place on the ground to land, stop the horse, and do exactly the reverse to mounting. Be sure both of your boots are loose in the stirrup, then dismount landing on the ground standing beside the left shoulder of the horse facing the rear.

SOME PRECAUTIONS: When mounting and dismounting, place your horse in a position so his left side is up hill or have him on level ground. Always mount from the uphill side. Riding-stock, trained to be mounted from either side, are a definite advantage. Be sure to keep your shoe in the stirrup **only** to the ball of the foot.

Ideal footwear for riding is a boot with a heel and a slick sole. Cowboy boots or packer type boots with slick or mini-lug soles are best. **NEVER** ride in tennis shoes. This type of shoe will easily slip all the way through a stirrup and you can get hung up in a very precarious position. Tapaderos will prevent your foot from going through the stirrup and they provide protection to the foot from rain, snow, cold, etc. The downside is they add additional weight to your saddle.

It is recognized that boots with heavy lug soles are often used for riding because this is standard footwear for working or hunting. Special precautions must be exercised when riding with lug soles, especially when dismounting. It is very easy to get hung up in the stirrup at the worst possible time.

Reining

It is important to recognize that the bit in the horse's mouth has a design that gives a prying leverage on the horse's jaw. Proper use of the reins calls for just enough pressure to serve as a signal to the horse. Too much pressure is distressful to the horse and is dangerous to the rider. Excessive pulling on the reins may force the horse to back up and be dangerously out of control, or it may cause him to rear over backwards. Many serious injuries have been caused in this manner.

To direct the horse forward, the signal is given by leaning slightly forward in the saddle, making a clicking sound, and then by applying pressure with the heel. A light touch is usually sufficient. A harder kick is sometimes needed with a less sensitive animal. The amount of persuasion necessary is usually learned through trial and error.

Turning the animal is accomplished in one of two ways, neck reining or direct reining. Direct reining involves pulling on the rein and leaning slightly in the saddle in the direction you wish to travel. Animals that neck rein must be trained to do so. If the horse is to turn left, hold both reins in the left hand and move this hand to the left. Press the reins (lightly at first) on the right side of his neck and lean in the saddle slightly to the left.

To stop the horse, say "whoa" and lightly pull on the reins and lean in the saddle to the rear. As soon as he has stopped, release the rein pressure and sit up straight. Be alert at all times and keep your back straight and your feet in the stirrups, just to the ball of the foot. Move your hips with the horse and keep your upper body straight and still. All horses do not rein the same, as this is largely a function of how much (or how little) training the animal has received in the past.

Some animals, especially mules, may require a little more persuasion known as "plow reining." This amounts to medium to heavy direct pressure (pulling) on the rein in the direction you want the animal to turn, with the left hand pulling the left rein, and the right hand pulling the right rein.

Leading a Pack String

All horses do not make good lead horses (most often referred to as the "string horse"). As with people, some are leaders and some are followers. Generally, the more dominant horse should be the lead or "string horse." A string horse must walk along without reacting to every new situation along the route. When leading an animal while riding, hold the lead rope in your right hand and your reins in your left hand. Keep the rope free of the saddle and saddle parts (saddle bag, rain coat, etc.) as well as your feet to eliminate danger of becoming entangled with it in case the pack animals become unruly. Experienced horsemen, at times, use the horn of the saddle to lead by. This is done by wrapping the lead rope one turn counter-clockwise around the horn and holding the end of it with the right hand, or tucking it under your right leg.

Remember!! NEVER tie the lead rope to the horn of your saddle or make a solid loop in the end of the lead rope and hook it over the saddle horn. If it is necessary to have the right hand free for a few moments, either shift the lead rope into the left hand without the wrap around the horn, or make a wrap and tuck the end under the right leg.

The main dangers of leading a pack mule while riding are (1) getting yourself tangled up in the lead rope; (2) getting the lead rope under your saddle horse's tail; (3) getting the lead rope tangled up in the saddle bags

The Pigtail is fastened to the rigging rings on each side of the pack saddle.

or rain gear; (4) getting the saddle horse tangled up; (5) getting the lead pack mule tangled; or (6) pinching your finger between the saddle horn and lead rope when your pack animals pull back. Dropping your lead rope is embarrassing and has some potential of leading to a wreck or a runaway pack train.

Keep excess slack out of the rope (about three feet is a good average), so your horse cannot step over it, especially with a hind foot. Never allow the lead rope to be below your horse's hock. This will also keep the lead pack mule from stepping over the lead rope. Use your arm to maneuver the lead rope to keep it out from under your horse's tail. Watch this particularly when traveling around switchbacks on the trail. If your horse gets the rope under his tail, stop him. If he will not raise his tail and release the rope, get off and lift his tail up and let the rope drop. If the rope is drawn through while the tail is clamped down on it, it will burn the horse and he will likely become unruly. A horse that has been burned is nervous about a recurrence. If flies are bad, it may be impossible to keep your horse from switching his tail over the rope. In this situation, it is best to wipe your stock with a good horse fly repellent.

CAUTION!! NEVER use human insect repellent on horses. It may cause them to lose their hair. If horse fly repellent is not available, another method is to just tie your horse's tail to the saddle string on the left side. If the situation is really troublesome, this stunt might save you from getting hurt. Be sure you untie the tail when you reach your destination and before you loosen the saddle cinch.

The safest way to fasten the lead rope of one pack mule to the mule in front is to tie the lead rope into the breakaway of the pigtail. The pigtail is fastened to the rigging rings on each side of the pack saddle. The breakaway should be made of a rope that will break with a pull of about 300 to 400 pounds (a ⅜-inch diameter, three-strand composite rope pigtail with ¼ inch Manila breakaway is good). This will prevent injury to any more than one mule if one animal should fall or pull back, and yet provide reliable control under normal travel conditions. Leave enough slack in the middle of the rope, where it passes over the top of the saddle, to allow it to be doubled back through the rear D-ring of the saddle tree. Extend it about one foot to the rear. An overhand knot tied in the doubled rope makes a loop over the pack animal's hips for the manila breakaway that the next mules lead rope is tied into. A good (maybe better) alternative is a specially tied pigtail knot called a "fish knot". Most saddle makers can tie this knot. It is not a recommended practice to tie the pigtail or breakaway to the rear bow on the packsaddle. This can cause the saddle to be pulled sideways when the mule behind pulls to the right or left. The knot to use in the lead rope for pigtailing pack stock together is illustrated in Chapter Nine.

NEVER tie a lead rope to light saddle parts such as saddle strings or breeching straps. You will only tear up equipment. It is a good idea to equip even your riding saddles with pigtails and a breakaway.

Leave just enough slack in the lead rope to allow the horse being led to drink at a creek crossing, but not enough that he might step over it.

Problems often arise when a pack string is stopped or just starting out, so try to keep moving once they are lined out. Always speak to your pack animals before starting to move. A simple "mules", or "heads up donks", or a whistle will alert them that you are moving on and this will greatly reduce unnecessary broken breakaways.

A steady three miles per hour is a good pace. You should travel only as fast as your slowest pack animal.

Carrying Tools

It is not safe to try to hand-carry things on a horse. It is always dangerous to try to mount an animal with something being carried on your back or in your hand. This disrupts your balance, you may spook the horse, and/or you may fall on the item being carried. If you must carry a rifle, a tool, or any other article, use a scabbard, or try to tie it onto the saddle in such a way that it cannot possibly become loose, and cannot chafe or hang against you or your horse. Be sure all sharp edges are well sheathed. If you cannot tie your tool on the saddle, mount your horse first, then have someone cautiously hand you the tool. If your horse shows fear of the tool, do not take it on the horse. If you are alone, place the tool on a log, stump, fence, or someplace where you can reach it, then mount, ride to it and take it, providing your horse does not object. Once again, mounting with a tool, knapsack, or even a lunch bucket in hand is not recommended. Permanent, painful, and costly accidents are on record from this dangerous practice. It is safer to tie packsacks, etc., to the saddle horn or put them on a pack mule than it is to wear them.

Manners

Probably the most important, although most abused, safety factor in use of stock can be called behavior or manners. Behavior and manners apply to both horse and rider. Some horses may develop a habit of trying to follow others too closely. When this happens, the horse or mules ahead may become unnecessarily unruly which could cause a wreck, or the animal ahead may kick and injure your horse. It is your responsibility to keep your horse back. Likewise, traveling too slow and impeding those behind is bad manners. If you cannot make your horse keep up, pull out of line and let others go by until you **"fit in."**

Always respect the position of the other person while you are maneuvering around or working horses or mules. If another person is working with an animal, be sure to approach on the same side the person is standing. Never approach the other side unless both man and animal are expecting you to and unless you have a good reason. Do not forget to speak to the animal if you come within working distance.

Be mindful of other riders and their horses in the handling of your horse. **A good horseman never starts out before other members of the party are ready to ride**. If one rider dismounts to open a gate, move an obstacle from the trail, or for any other reason, other horsemen should respect his action by waiting for him to mount and have his horse under control before resuming the journey.

Most horses and mules are easily frightened by someone approaching rapidly from behind. A warning of intention to ride up to a party, given at a distance, and an orderly approach is the proper method.

I'll make one last comment on safety. **DOGS AND MULES DO NOT MIX!** Leave your dog at home. Although your dog and your stock may get along fine, this cannot be guaranteed with other stock. In a confrontation usually one of two things will occur, neither of which is a good option. Either you will have a dead dog (many mules instinctively will attack and attempt to kill a dog) or there will be one heck of a wreck with possible injury to humans and/or stock.

Chasing these critters is what got me into packing!

CHAPTER FOUR

STOCK BEHAVIOR
Ten Qualities of a Horses Mind

The very things about equine (horses, donkeys, and therefore mules) that can cause us trouble with their behavior are the very characteristics that have kept them in existence for thousands of years. A crucial concept to understand about horses (when I say horses I am also referring to mules) is the fact that they are a **prey species**. They have been on the food chain of predators (big cats and big dogs) for eons. In order for the species to survive, they have developed several instinctive traits that are imbedded genetically and are "just always there". When a horse is under mental or physical pressure, these instincts can kick in and any previous training may be temporarily forgotten.

Each species of animal has mental and behavioral characteristics that are unique to that species. In order to effectively control behavior in the horse we must understand these instinctive qualities and the subtle "body language" that can clue us into just what they are thinking at a particular moment. The Natural Horsemanship Movement that has surfaced in the past decade or so recognizes these instinctive traits. Many professional horse trainers today have developed training techniques based on these natural instincts and body language. It is well established that these persuasive training methods can work more rapidly and are more effective than the traditional coercive (Powder River – Let Her Buck) methods.

So let's examine ten qualities of a horse or mule's mind that will help us understand just why they do what they do. Remember, many of these qualities are a direct result of the fact that the horse is a prey species. Man is the ultimate predator! (Much of the information for this chapter is from a video by Robert M. Miller, DVM. This 2 hour and 15 minute video titled *Understanding Horses* is available from Smiling Pinto Station, A Division of Video Velocity, P.O. Box K, Virginia City NV, 89440.)

1. The first and foremost instinctive quality of a horse or mule is the fact that they are a **flight creature**. Their number one survival mechanism is to flee from danger. This trait is unique to the horse. No other domestic animal has this quality as their primary survival mechanism. Everything about a horse or mule's behavior comes back to this! If they are frightened, their natural instinct is to **run away from danger**. Their secondary survival behavior is to fight, which for a horse means to strike, bite, or kick.

2. Another significant quality of the horse is their **extreme perceptivity**. The five senses of the horse (sight, hearing, touch, smell, and taste) are finely tuned, far superior to that of a human. The unique function and large size of their eye allows for immediate focus and the ability to pick up motion at great distances. They have superb night vision and excellent peripheral vision. The location of the eyes at the side of the head allows for 360 degree coverage with very little head movement. Also, the eyes see independently, allowing the horse to see to the front and to the rear at the same time. A horse's hearing is better than ours, mainly because they have large, directional ears. Their sense of smell is almost as good as a dog's sense of smell. This sense can tell a horse many things about its immediate environment of which we are often unaware. Their sense of touch is finely developed and they can easily determine the confidence or tenseness of a rider, right through the saddle and pad.

The highly perceptive nature of horses can give us problems because they often react to things we humans often do not sense. With a better understanding of this quality, possibly, we will not be so quick to chastise our horse for some perceived bad behavior without just cause. Smart hunters will use this enhanced perceptivity to their advantage as horses and mules will often spot game long before the hunter.

3. Horses are **fast learners**. In the wild, slow learners do not survive. As a rule, three experiences, good or bad, and a horse learns and never forgets. It is important to generalize the same learning experience in several locations, however. I learned this concept the hard way one time when I bought a horse tied to a post. This was a good, sound, gentle horse, seemingly perfect in every way. I turned the horse out in a large

This mule sees and hears to the rear with the right eye and ear and forward with the left eye and ear.

open pasture and was unable to catch him again until I ran him into a smaller round pen. In the round pen he made the classic two laps, stopped, and faced me. He was no problem to catch at that point. This horse had been trained to catch only in a round pen and was impossible to catch in an open pasture. The ability to learn quickly is an obvious advantage during the training phase. Again, three experiences in multiple locations and horses learn very quickly!

4. Horses have a very **fast reaction time**. Faster than any other domestic animal. Prey species that did not react quickly to danger would not survive. If a horse truly wants to get you, with a strike, kick or bite, you won't see it coming and you won't be able to get out of the way if you are within range. Also, a frightened horse can hurt you without meaning to harm you. Always try to stand in a safe position at the shoulder of the animal while attempting to halter, saddle, bridle, pick up feet, etc. Most people are injured by gentle horses that make sudden movements.

5. The horse can be **desensitized** to things that frighten them. This is obviously a good quality, however it is a key step in a horse's development we often fail to take, or we fail to complete. Failure to

desensitize to the things that frighten them can result in stock that have bad habits and become unsafe. Training during the imprinting period at birth is the easiest and most effective method of habituating stock to frightening stimuli. Unfortunately, we do not have this opportunity available to us if we are buying stock at three to ten years of age. Two other forms of desensitization are referred to as "flooding" and "progressive desensitization". **Flooding** involves endlessly repeating a fearful experience until the fear is gone. This is obviously easier on a young foal than on a full grown horse. **Progressive desensitization** takes longer but by working the horse gradually toward a fearful stimulus and using the advance and retreat technique, fears of the horse can be overcome. Giving a small food reward each time the horse accepts the frightening stimuli greatly aids this training process.

6. The horse has an **excellent memory**. Horses never forget any sensory experience, good or bad. Fortunately horses can be taught to tolerate a bad experience. The key is to train properly at an early age.

7. The horse is **easily dominated and accepts leadership**. In the wild, horses depend on flight to survive, and they always run (flee) together in a band lead by a pack leader. The pack leader is usually an old

Physical strength has nothing to do with establishing dominance and assuming leadership over a horse or mule.

mare. With pack leadership, it's seniority that is important, not gender or physical strength. The stallion owns the herd, but the mare will be the pack leader because she has lived long enough and has the wisdom and experience to lead the band to safety. Stallions come and go on a regular basis. In a domestic herd, a gelding can become the pack leader just as readily as the mare. Physical strength has nothing to do with leadership of a band of horses or of a single horse. Horses respect leadership and leadership comes from control of movement. This is why children or adults of small stature are able to handle large horses just as easily as the macho cowboy.

8. The horse has its **own body language**. In order to effectively communicate with the horse we should understand their body language. This is especially useful in a round pen training situation. Body language such as the elevated head which signals fear or flight, or the lowered head combined with varying degrees of licking and chewing which signals submissiveness or acceptance, are very useful in the training mode. Numerous books and videos are available which fully explain this trait.

9. Horses exhibit a **dominance hierarchy**. Movement is life to a horse, and dominance of one horse over another is established by control of movement. This can be in the form of causing movement, or preventing movement, i.e., flight control. Humans establish their dominance and leadership over horses through this same behavior of controlling flight.

10. The horse is a **precocial species**. Again being a prey species, and a species that relies on flight for survival, it is essential that the newborn foal be **fully developed at birth**, i.e., precocial. Being fully developed at birth allows the newborn to flee a predator shortly after birth. Their senses are fully developed, and therefore, their **ability to learn is fully developed**. This is why the best time to train a horse or mule is immediately upon birth and within the first three to five days of life.

The ability to handle the ears, pick up feet, or tolerate handling of any kind is far easier to teach at this time (during the imprinting period), than at any other time of a horses life. This is not to say they can't be taught later in life, it is just made much easier if they are exposed to handling of all kinds at a very early age. This training during the imprinting period must be done correctly, however, or the foal may develop bad habits. Many books and tapes are available to you to help you learn this procedure correctly.

Understanding these ten qualities of a horses mind can help us address problems with equine behavior. It can help us be safer as we work around these animals, and it will make us more proficient in our overall stock handling ability.

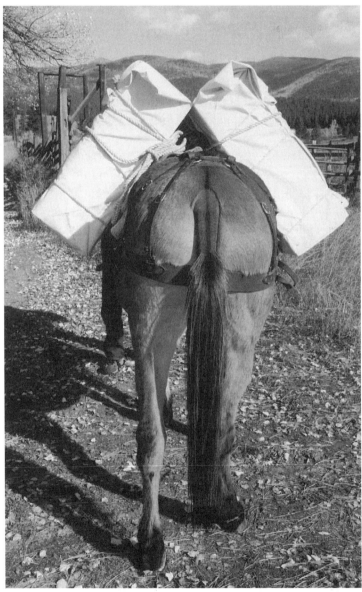

Traditional Decker loads are positioned to form an "A" over the pack mule's back.

CHAPTER FIVE

DECKER PHILOSOPHY
Saddles, Pads, and Tack

I have already mentioned the durability, versatility, and humane nature of the Decker Saddle that allows heavier loads to be packed with less wear and tear on pack stock. Also, greater varieties and shapes of cargo can be accommodated, and the loads can be balanced quicker and easier with the Decker than with other packing styles. The need to pack heavy, bulky, loads in rough, mountainous, terrain is what prompted the development of the Decker. Packing these heavier, bulkier loads resulted in a need to provide for maximum protection of the pack animal.

Although numerous variations are possible, traditional Decker Style packing consists of two loads of similar weight and bulk that are wrapped in a piece of canvas called a mantie. These cargoed or mantied loads are tied with rope to each side of the saddle utilizing a "basket hitch". The two loads are positioned to form an "A" over the back and down each side of the pack mule. In most packing situations the loads should be allowed to "swing freely" at the bottom, although, certain packing situations may require them to be tied down. The ability of each side-pack to "swing freely" is a major point of difference between Decker Style and Sawbuck Style Packing. This ability of the load to swing freely allows the mule to breathe easier, as opposed to loads that are tied solidly down with a diamond hitch as is we often see on a Sawbuck. Additionally, on a Decker the load can move and then settle back into place if it encounters a bumper tree or some other solid object. On a Sawbuck, when an immovable force (the mule and load) meets an immovable object (a tree) something has to give. This results in added wear and tear on the mule and/or the pack. As with all packing styles, balancing the load to keep the saddle centered on the animal's back is essential.

Stock in good physical condition should be expected to carry 20 percent of their body weight every packing day, throughout the season. This includes the weight of the saddle which is approximately 40 pounds.

The caption on this old photo reads ... "mule loaded with cook stove probably going to Moose Creek. The weight was balanced on either side...stove had to be lifted off every 2 hours. The mule wasn't much good after that."

A mule weighing 1,100 pounds is capable of carrying a 180 pound payload on every trip, or 90 pounds per side. Actually a mule is capable of carrying as much as the packer can put on them. However, overloading can take years off of the mule's life, even to the point of ruining a mule in a single trip depending on the actual weight and distance traveled.

Sawbuck packing with panniers and a top pack is an excellent packing system and it has been for centuries. To say this is not a valid packing system would be ludicrous! However, I believe the Decker packing system offers several advantages to both packer and pack animal making it a superior system. Several significant traits of the Decker Saddle and Decker Packing Style which gives this system a distinct advantage over other packing styles are:

1. Steel bows rather than wooden crossbucks produce a stronger more durable saddle tree.

2. Wooden bars of the Decker saddle tree can be rasped and shaped to fit the back of each individual pack animal.

3. The saddle rigging is fully adjustable from a full rigging to center fire. This allows the cinch to be placed in the proper location, irregardless of the conformation of the pack animal.

4. The Decker Saddle uses a single cinch. A Sawbuck uses three - a double cinch to hold the saddle in place, as well as a lash cinch used for tying on top loads.

5. A canvas and leather halfbeed with wooden pack boards on the side provides excellent protection to the pack animal from the load being carried. The pack board distributes the weight across the animal's side rather than allowing pressure in one small location which can irritate or injure the animal.

6. Loads that are cargoed and swung from the Decker Saddle are carried in a more comfortable position higher on the animal's back. Panniers on a Sawbuck are carried much lower and ride on the rib cage of the pack animal. More efficient positioning of the load allows the animal to carry more weight.

7. Two side-packs of significantly different weight can easily be balanced and packed on the Decker by setting the heavy side higher and the lighter side lower. When using panniers, the sides need to be relatively even in weight so the load will balance.

8. Load adjustments to keep the saddle positioned properly on the animal's back can be made literally in seconds with the Decker system.

5-3 – Equipment cost (in 2005) per pack animal will be $800-$1,000.

With these advantages in mind, let's now discuss the equipment necessary to become outfitted in the Decker Packing Style. The components necessary are 1) a halter, 2) a pad, 3) manties and cargo ropes, and 4) a Decker saddle, see figure 5-3.

The Pack Halter

Many different styles of halters exist, some good, some not so good. As mentioned in Chapter Three, all halters must be strong. They must be relatively lightweight, maintenance free, and affordable. When buying a halter, it is important to know if it is for a horse or a mule. A major trait of a mule is their strong survival instinct, consequently, mules generally will not step where they cannot see. This is why I prefer a "side pull" style of halter, figure 5-4, as opposed to a center pull halter, figure 5-5. The side pull halter allows the mule to turn his head and look at the ground, even when he is tied to the rear of another mule and being pulled rather briskly. This feature will greatly reduce the number of broken pigtails while traveling on a trail with a string of mules. A standard center pull type halter generally works just fine on a horse.

A good mule halter (and the style I prefer) is made of 1½ inch or 1¾ inch harness leather. It will have a roller buckle on the left side and a

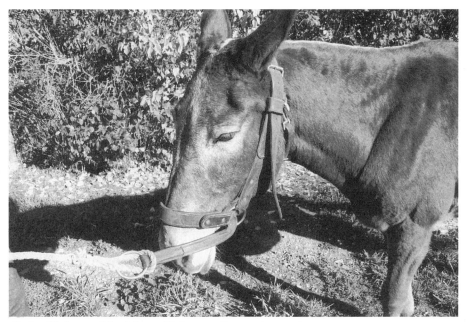

5-4 – *Halter with side-pull draw allows the mule to turn his head and see where he is stepping. The lead is attached with an eye splice, not a snap!*

5-5 – *This halter has several features that I do not recommend. It has a center pull rather than side pull, it's made of chain rather than leather, and it has a snap and multi-braided rope.*

5-6 – This is a good rope halter for riding stock; no buckles and no snaps! Note proper tie of halter.

snap on the throatlatch. Rings are used to assemble the headstall and a ring is attached at the end of the side draw for a place to attach the lead rope. The lead rope should be a twelve foot long piece of ½ inch diameter, three-strand composite, eye spliced on one end and back spliced on the other. (Other types of rope will work but I prefer the three-strand composite.) The rope is attached to the halter using the eye splice at the draw ring. DO NOT USE A SNAP TO ATTACH YOUR LEAD ROPE TO THE HALTER! A snap at this point is a weak link and a definite safety hazard! All hardware should be stainless steel or brass. Stay away from chrome plated pot metal, it will break under pressure.

A similarly constructed halter, but with a "chain draw", is sometimes used to teach hard to pull or "pull back" mules to lead. This is a good training tool, but switch to the leather draw as soon as the mule is properly trained to lead. Keep in mind the strength of the halter. Lightweight show halters will generally not hold up over time. Cotton halters can become weak from rot without you knowing it. Halters with a lot of chain and big nosebands can add unnecessary weight. Flat nylon halters are fine however my preference in a rope halter is climbing rope. The climbing rope halter is very strong, lightweight, adjustable, and there are no buckles or snaps to break.

Pack Pads

The pack pad is a very important piece of equipment that protects the pack animal from the saddle and the load that is placed on him. A good pad will exhibit several very important features. 1) The pad must be big enough (a pad in the 30" X 40" range works well), and it must be thick enough to provide adequate protection. A pad must often serve as a "gasket" to accommodate a poor fitting saddle. 2) The pad must be absorbent to wick sweat away from the pack mule, and it must be of a material that will cause only minimal heat buildup. Overheating is a major cause of the dreaded "white marks" that often appear on the back or withers area of dark, solid colored animals. Excessive heat damages the hair follicles, which causes the hair to turn white. This is not harmful to the animal. However, it can be (and should be) embarrassing to the packer. 3) Pads should not wrinkle, nor should they slip or creep while on an animal's back. 4) Pads must not harbor bacteria or fungus and it is essential that they be washable.

Pads should always be kept as clean as possible. Never allow a pad to lie on the ground. Sweat and dirt become caked on a pad after every use. I routinely brush my pads every time I saddle, even when saddling ten animals. Dirty or worn out pads can cause unnecessary hair loss on an animal's back. Keep pads clean and replace them when they are worn out!

Manties and Cargo Ropes

Cargoing or mantying allows the packer versatility in the size and weight of the load. It also provides a maximum amount of adjustment for balancing the load on the pack saddle. The manties and ropes provide convenient additional pieces of camp equipment such as covers for saddles or other camp equipment, and especially as bed roll covers. Cargo ropes have many uses such as securing tents, hanging food in bear country, building rope corrals, or picketing stock.

Two manties are required to pack a Decker Saddle. Manties are traditionally made of seven foot by seven foot or seven foot by eight foot pieces of canvas. Six foot by six foot manties are too small for most loads, and eight foot by eight foot manties are a little big and cumbersome. I would, however, rather have them too big than too small. I prefer a 14-15 ounce, untreated, white, canvas. Ten ounce canvas is too light and flimsy, and 18 ounce canvas is heavier than necessary. Also, 18 ounce canvas is stiff and difficult to work with. Treated canvas (water repellent) has an annoying odor that permeates anything wrapped in it. Treated canvas also does not breathe and game meat wrapped in it can spoil. Other fabrics may be acceptable as manties; however, canvas is traditional and it works just fine for me.

Two cargo ropes are also necessary to pack a Decker. Many types of rope can be used as a cargo rope, i.e., Manila, polypropylene, braided nylon, composite, cotton, etc. A cargo rope should be cut 35 feet long and then be eye spliced on the working end and back spliced on the running end. A three strand rope is required to eye splice and back splice. A cargo rope should be ⅜ inch in diameter. Quarter inch rope is too hard to hang on to, and ½ inch rope is unnecessary for the task. My preference is a 35-foot, ⅜ inch diameter, three-strand, composite rope.

The Decker Pack Saddle

The Decker Saddle consists of numerous basic parts. These parts are: the tree, a half-breed and quarter-breed, a spider, breeching, breast collar, rigging, cinch, on/off-side latigos, and two sling ropes. The anatomy of the Decker Saddle is illustrated in figure 5-7 on page 57.

The **tree** is the foundation of the Decker saddle. It is made up of two steel bows (often referred to as Dees, or D-rings) and two wooden bars, preferably made from cottonwood. Other woods have been tried but cottonwood always stands out as best due to its resistance to splitting and the fact it is relatively light weight for a hardwood. Also, cottonwood can be easily shaped with a wood rasp. In spite of the advantages of cottonwood, the downside is it may not be as readily available as other woods such as pine. Tree manufactures today often use pine, so the buyer may not have a choice in the matter. Rings, buckles, or straps are attached to the bars so the breast collar, rigging, and lazy straps can be attached to the tree.

Many attempts have been made to improve on the original design of the "OPR" Decker tree. Although I try to keep an open mind about these sorts of things, this is one place where the saying "if it ain't broke, don't fix it" really fits. Some attempts at modifying the Decker tree have been well intentioned. On some models the bows have been reshaped to accommodate pannier bags, basically turning the Decker into a Sawbuck saddle. Attempts have been made to make "one size fits all" trees by adding a swivel point between the bar and the bow. Bars on some trees are made of fiberglass which can't be shaped to individual mule's backs.

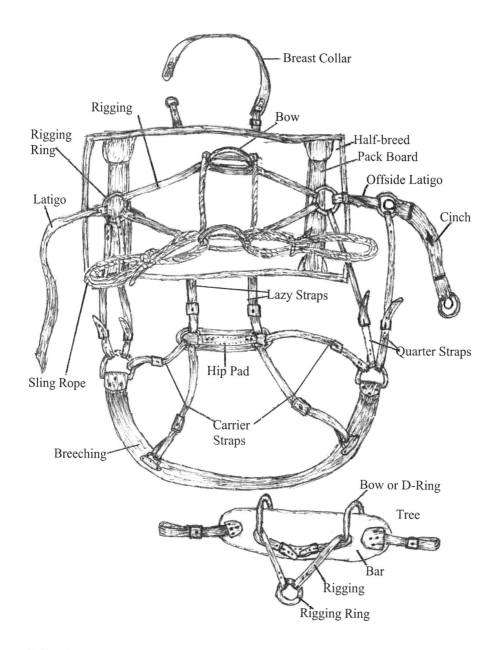

*5-7 – **Anatomy of the Decker Pack Saddle.** You should be familiar with these parts.*

Depending on how often you go packing and how much weight you pack, any of these changes could work just fine for you, assuming quality workmanship. My preference however will always be the traditional style tree and saddle.

The **halfbreed** is a covering over the saddle designed to protect the pack animal from the load. It traditionally is made of canvas and leather and is stuffed with bear grass or horse hair. Today many saddle makers use artificial hog hair (furniture stuffing). Two wooden pack boards are fixed on either side of the halfbreed near the bottom edges. These serve to spread the weight of the load across the entire rib area rather than impact and possibly injure one small spot. A **quarterbreed** or halfbreed cover is nothing more than a light covering designed to protect the halfbreed. The halfbreed is a rather expensive component of the saddle, and the quarterbreed protects and extends the life of the halfbreed.

The **breeching** (most often pronounced "britchin'") is a component of the saddle with the primary function of holding the saddle from sliding forward. It is a three or four inch wide piece of leather that extends around the rump or haunch area of the animal. It is held in position by a **spider**, made up of a hip pad, four carrier straps, and two lazy straps. Four quarter straps, two on each side, hold the breeching to the rigging and cinch. Proper adjustment of the breeching is crucial and is discussed fully in Chapter Seven.

A fully adjustable **rigging** attaches to the tree and to the cinch to hold the saddle in place. The rigging can be adjusted to fit any pack animal's particular conformation so the cinch can always be in the proper location. A ⅜ inch diameter composite pigtail rope is eye spliced to the rigging ring on either side. The center of this rope extends through the back bow to the rear and a loop is made in the rope with an over hand knot or a Fish Knot. A quarter inch Manila breakaway is attached to the loop in the pigtail.

The **breast collar** extends around the chest of the pack animal. It is hooked solid to the tree on the right side and hooked with a snap on the left side. The breast collar keeps the saddle from sliding backward when traveling uphill or when an animal that is tied on behind pulls back.

Cinches for a horse or mule are like belts on people. Each has their own size and they must be measured to fit. There is a perfect flat spot on either side of all horses and mules, just behind the elbow. From the point of the elbow the center of this flat spot is roughly six inches back and two inches up. The rings of the cinch should lie on these flat spots to prevent a sore from developing. A good pack cinch is a 19 to 21 strand, diamond-stitched Mohair cinch with stainless steel or cadmium buckles. Pack cinches have a second smaller ring inside the main cinch ring that is used for tying loads down. Cinches should be made of wool or Mohair to allow for maximum air flow and cooling. Cinches must be kept as clean as possible. Cinches that become dirty, hard, or matted can cause sores.

The **latigo** is a strap of No. 1 grade latigo leather, approximately 3/32 of an inch thick. The latigo should be 1¼ inches wide by six feet long and tapered to ½ inch at the outer end. The latigos, one on each side join the cinch to the rigging ring.

The final components of the Decker Saddle are the **sling ropes**, sometimes referred to as "swing" ropes. My preference for a sling rope is ½ inch diameter, three-strand composite, 24 feet to 28 feet long. This rope is eye spliced on one end and back spliced on the other. Both ropes are attached to the front bow of the saddle and "put up" on the rear bow.

Decker Pack Saddles that are kept clean, well oiled, and well maintained can be expected to last a packer's lifetime.

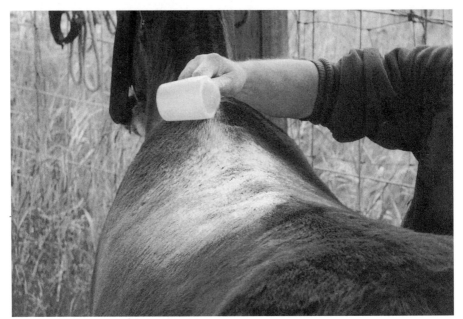

6-1-a – Sprinkle a thin, even layer of flour over the animal's back where the tree will set.

6-1-b – Lightly wet the bars.

CHAPTER SIX

FITTING THE DECKER PACK SADDLE

A distinct advantage of a Decker Pack Saddle is the ability to fully adjust the saddle to properly fit each individual animal. The two components that can and should be adjusted are the tree, and the rigging. Fitting the tree and rigging to your pack animal's back is very important to stabilize the load and to provide comfort to the animal. A saddle that does not fit properly will often lean to the side or result in uncomfortable pressure points. This can lead to turned loads, soared animals, or even major wrecks.

Fitting the Tree

To properly fit a tree to an animal's back you must first disassemble the saddle so you have just the tree in hand. Sprinkle a thin, even layer of flour over the animal's back where the tree will set. Lightly wet the bars of the tree with a damp cloth, now set the tree in the proper position on the animal's back. The bars of the tree should fit against the rear portion of the shoulder blades, not on top of them. Push straight down on the tree to resemble a load on the saddle, now lift the tree straight up and off of the animal's back. Turn the tree over and you will have an exact impression of how well (or how poorly) the tree fits. (See 6-1, a-f)

If the flour uniformly covers the entire bottom surface of the bars, you have a perfect fit. If there are gaps in the coverage, or maybe only the lower half or top half of the bar is covered, then you will need to rasp off a portion of the wooden bar to make it fit. A good wood rasp or a worn out shoeing rasp works great for this step. Simply rasp off some wood in the areas covered by the flour. Take a little wood off each time, and repeat the process until the proper coverage is achieved.

6-1-c – Set the tree in proper position and press down.

6-1-d – Lift tree straight up and off.

6-1-e – Turn tree over and check fit.

6-1-f – Rasp off high spots, repeat process until proper fit is achieved.

The quality of your tree will have a direct bearing on the success of the tree fitting process. This personalized fit cannot be achieved with trees made of fiberglass. Also, if the bolts that attach the bows to the bars have not been counter sunk and the holes filled with quality wood filler, you will not be able to rasp over the metal bolt head. If your saddle tree looks like this, plan on investing in a very good pad. (See photo, page 65)

Adjusting the Rigging

Proper adjustment of the rigging is important to both hold the saddle in the correct position and to keep it from causing a sore or hair loss on the animal. To adjust the rigging, it is important to follow this sequence (see photos, pages 66-70):

1. Place the pad and saddle in the correct position on the animal's back, see figures 6-3, a & b.

2. Fasten the cinch. If the cinch is the proper length, the center of the cinch ring on each side should be approximately six inches in back of the elbow and about two inches above the elbow, figures 6-3, c & d.

3. Set the breeching in place, figure 6-3, e.

4. Starting with the hip pad, adjust the two lazy straps so the hip pad is positioned half way between the highest point of the croup and the base of the tail, figure 6-3, f.

5. Now adjust the four carrier straps so the breeching is about four inches below the rear most point of the rump. Tip the D-ring ends of the breeching up slightly so the breeching matches the slope of the haunch. This will help prevent cutting hair at the top of the breeching strap, figures 6-3, g & h.

6. Adjust the four quarter straps, two on each side, so the breeching is tightened within about four inches of the haunch when the breeching is pulled to the rear. (Your hand turned sideways is about four inches.) Figure 6-3, i.

7. Snap the breast collar in place and adjust it so you can slip your hand (knuckles against the chest) between the chest and the breast collar. The collar must be loose enough to allow the animal to put its head to the ground without choking, and it must be tight enough so it does not drape over the point of the shoulder where it can impede shoulder movement or rub off a spot of hair, figure 6-3, j.

Poor tree construction. Bolt heads are not counter-sunk deep enough. Bow attachment extends above the bar. Ropes will hang up and wear on this protrusion.

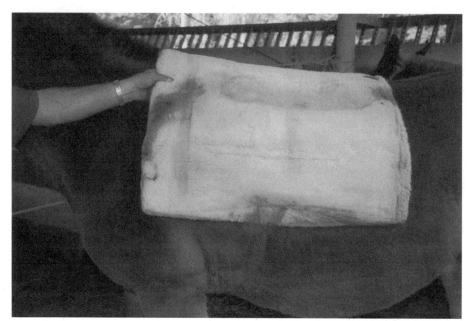

6-3-a – Initial position of pad should be forward to line up with front of leg.

6-3-b – Position saddle so bars of the tree lie just behind the shoulder blade.

6-3-c – Tighten cinch. Rigging ring should be half on and half below the bottom edge of the pack board. Ring in the picture is too low and must be adjusted.

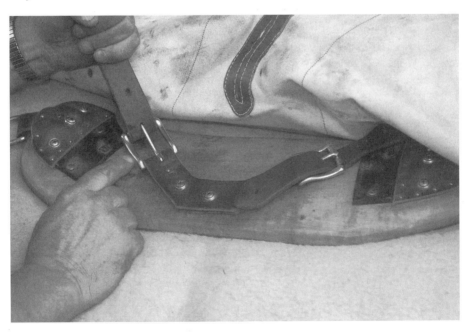

6-3-d – Buckles attached to tree are used to adjust rigging.

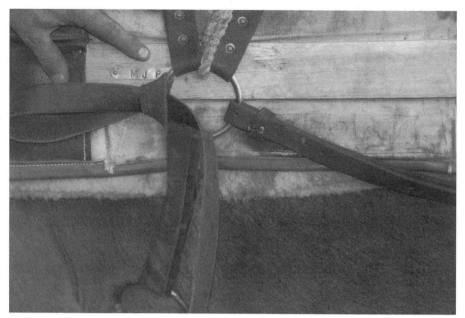

6-3-e – Correct position of rigging ring. Tie latigo with a side slip knot. Set breeching in place.

6-3-f – Adjust two lazy straps so hip pad is halfway between the top of the croup and base of the tail.

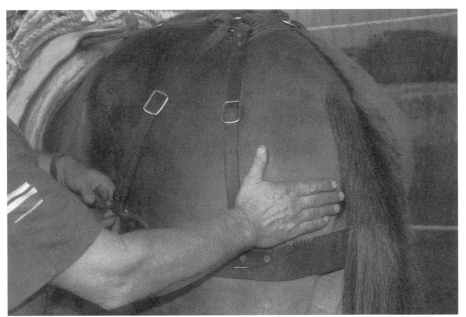

6-3-g – Adjust the four carrier straps so the breeching is about four inches below the rear most point of the rump.

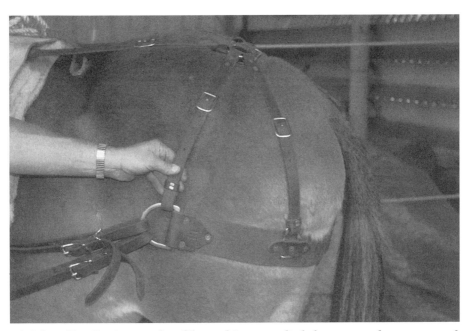

6-3-h – Tip D-ring ends of breeching up slightly to match contour of haunch.

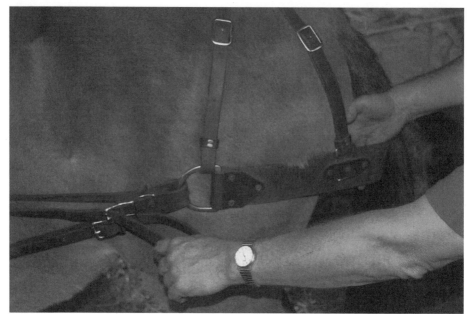

6-3-i – Adjust quarter straps so breeching is tightened within about four inches of the haunch.

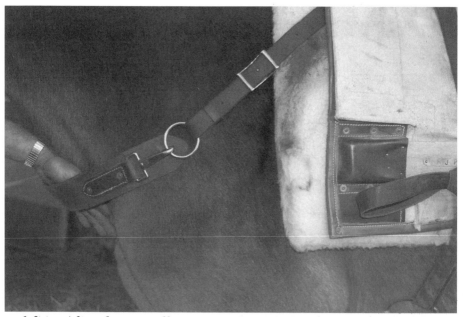

6-3-j – Adjust breast collar so your hand fits flat between the collar and the chest.

At this point your saddle is fully adjusted and should only require minor tweaking to achieve a perfect fit. Improper adjustment is most often indicated by "hair cutting" and/or creation of small bald spots or sores. Remember, as with humans, a horse or mule's body weight and shape can change slightly over the course of a season, so always keep an eye out for proper fit and adjust as needed.

Cargoing would prevent this horse from dining while en route.

CHAPTER SEVEN

CARGOING

This is where the artistry of Decker Style Packing begins. The goal of cargoing is to securely wrap two bundles that can be slung from each side of the Decker Saddle. These bundles must be cargoed in a standardized manner so they are tightly wrapped and the payload is protected from external forces such as dust, rain, or snow. Also, when packing stock feed (hay, hay cubes, pellets, grain), cargoing prevents the pack stock from attempting to eat from the loads en-route. Efficient cargoing requires the right equipment, an understanding of the theory of cargoing, and proper cargoing technique.

Equipment
Cargoing requires two manties and two ropes per pack animal. My preference in manties is 14 or 15 ounce white untreated canvas, seven feet by eight feet in size. The cargo rope I prefer is ⅜ inch diameter, three-strand composite. I like to cut cargo ropes 35 feet long, then eye splice one end and back splice the other. Other types of rope and other mantie materials are available that will likely work just fine. Canvas manties and three-strand composite cargo ropes are my preference, however.

Cargoing Theory
It is important to understand the theory of cargoing relative to load weight, load size, and distribution of weight within each side-pack. Each load will consist of two side-packs. If numerous items are to be cargoed, such as duffle or camp gear, it is always easier to "build" two sides at the same time. Spread two manties out and sort gear so, as closely as possible, equal weight and bulk are achieved in each side. If single items

of equal bulk and weight are to be cargoed, such as hay bales or sacks of grain, then building one side at a time would be appropriate.

As stated in Chapter Five, stock in good physical condition should be expected to carry 20 percent of their body weight every packing day throughout the season. An 1,100 pound mule should carry 220 pounds on every trip in order to achieve maximum efficiency. This will be 220 pounds minus 30 - 40 pounds for the saddle and 15 pounds for two manties and two ropes. This leaves us a 165-175 pound payload, or roughly 80 - 90 pounds per side. Having said all this, I want to emphasize the "20 percent of body weight formula" is only a guideline. Mules or horses are certainly capable of carrying more weight, and they will always appreciate carrying less weight. However, in order to be humane and fair to the pack animal (and the packer) it is important to try and limit the loads to this optimum weight (not maximum weight). Conversely, if we want to be efficient in our packing, we should strive for 20 percent of body weight each time we cargo a load.

Now let's discuss load size. As I've stated, one of the features of Decker Style Packing is we are not limited by the size of the pannier bag

Mule on left weighs 1,250 pounds. Mule on right weighs 1,000 pounds. Left mule can easily handle 250 pound load, right mule should only have 200 pound load.

or pack box. The overall size and bulk of our load requires careful consideration, however. If I were to pick an ideal size for each side-pack it would be close to 16 inches deep, by 22 inches wide, by 34 inches long. This is roughly the size of an average bale of hay. These dimensions can, and will vary considerably. The depth of a side-pack can range from ½ inch to about 24 inches. Width will vary from about 4 inches to roughly 24 inches, and length should be at least 30 inches to a maximum of 40 about inches.

The minimum dimensions are not as significant as the maximum dimensions. Standard clearing width for most back country trails is eight feet. Assuming the trail has been cleared (often times trails are cleared only every three to five years) we must consider our overall load width which will include both side-packs and the width of the pack animal. Most horses and mules are about two feet wide, and if our side-packs are each two feet deep, this will equal six feet. Now consider that the bottom inside corner of each side-pack extends approximately one foot away from the pack animal. The load is now eight feet wide. That's not much room for error, even on a well maintained trail. The half-breed is about 26 inches wide, therefore the width of the side-pack should be limited to about 24 inches. Packs that are more than 40 inches long will ride too

*This oversized load is long and awkward, but it **can** be packed on the Decker Saddle.*

low which is hard on the pack animal, and they will be more likely to bump or rub objects along the trail.

Although it may be possible to pack loads of any size or shape, it is much more difficult to balance loads with tiny side-packs or oversize side-packs. Strive for the happy medium or "ideal" size and the load will ride much better with less need for adjustment and less wear and tear on the pack animal.

A third important consideration when building loads is weight distribution within each side-pack. A good rule of thumb is to arrange items within each side-pack so the heaviest weight is one-third of the way down from the top of the load, and one-third of the way out from the back of the load. Obviously, this formula does not apply to uniform loads such as bales of hay. However, on loads of duffle, camp gear, or other loose items, it is a very important concept. The rationale of this load building strategy is that the heaviest portion of the side-pack will then rest on the tree of the saddle and the swing rope will attach the side-pack to the saddle directly over the heaviest part of the pack.

I should point out that some packers either do not understand this concept, or they just do not care about the well-being of their pack stock.

This load hangs much too low and places an unnecessary burden on the mule.

Loading side-packs with the heaviest weight in the bottom of the load will definitely limit the possibility of that saddle turning or rolling, but it is also much more difficult for pack stock to carry weight with the center of gravity on, or below their side. Think of yourself carrying a back pack. Would you rather have the weight up on your shoulders or down in the small of your back? Cargoing with weight distributed in the bottom of side-packs totally defeats a major advantage of the Decker system which is to be more humane to the pack animal!

One final comment on the theory of cargoing, fragile or expensive items within the side-pack must be arranged or protected so they are not damaged by tight cargo ropes or sling ropes, or by an occasional bump against a tree or other solid object.

Cargoing Technique

Cargoing is made easier if we utilize a standard and consistent technique. The technique described here will be used most of the time, but please understand, there will be exceptions depending on type of payload and size of the side-pack. Minor differences in technique will be experienced from packer to packer, although, the basic technique should remain consistent. Technique is a bit difficult to explain in writing, but when used in conjunction with the photos, the necessary steps should be apparent. Practice makes perfect!

1. Spread the mantie out flat. Grasp the mantie on one side with both hands, flip it up in the air, take one step backward and let go as the mantie settles to the ground. With a little practice you can achieve a properly positioned mantie with very little effort. There should be no wrinkles in the center portion of the mantie, figures 7-4, a & b.

2. Place the cargo diagonally and centered on the mantie, figure 7-4, c.

3. Slip your cargo rope into your belt or have it in your hand and drop it near the bottom of the load as you make the first fold of the canvas. The first fold comes directly from the bottom of the load toward the top of the load, similar to diapering a baby. Place your left knee on the folded canvas to hold it in place, figure 7-4, d.

4. With your left hand, reach across the load to the right side and grab the edge of the mantie approximately one foot out from the cargo. Pull ahead and to the left with this hand to form a **tight** corner at the **bottom, right edge** of the load, figure 7-4, e.

5. Now with your right hand, grab the same edge of the canvas about

18 inches beyond your left hand and pull upward and directly back toward the lower left corner of the load. Let go with the left hand and remove your knee as the canvas passes over the load. Pull the canvas tight along the right side of the load resulting in a **tight** corner along the **back and front, right edges** of the load. Step to the right side and face the load, then kneel and place both knees on the front side of the load. There should be a crease in the canvas flap that extends all the way across the front of the load, and this crease must be within two inches of the bottom of the load (not diagonal across the face of the load which is a common mistake.) Tuck the excess canvas under, even with the front-left side of the load, top to bottom, figure 7-4, f & g.

6. Repeat steps four and five on the left side of the load, remembering to interchange left and right, figures 7-4, h - j.

7. Straddle the load facing the top, and form a rain flap on top of the load by tucking each side in slightly and then folding the remaining canvas toward you, over the top. Leave short "ears" on the top left and right sides to shed rain. Fold excess canvas under to make a "clean" appearance. The crease of this fold should be 1/3 of the distance down from the top of the load. When you place the load on the saddle, the sling rope will be placed exactly at this crease, figures 7-4, k - m.

8. Throughout the cargoing process you must maintain pressure on the canvas and/or squeeze the load together with your legs in order to achieve a tight bundle.

9. Now step to the left side and kneel on the load to hold your mantie in place. The top of the pack will be on your left.

7-4-a

7-4-b

7-4-c

7-4-d

7-4-e

7-4-f

7-4-g

7-4-h

7-4-i

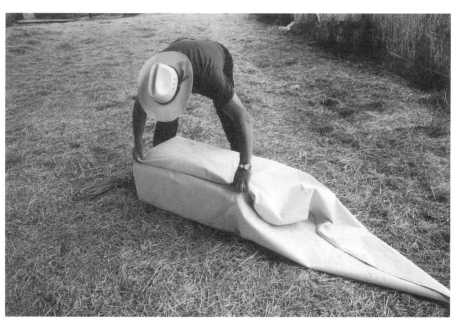

7-4-j

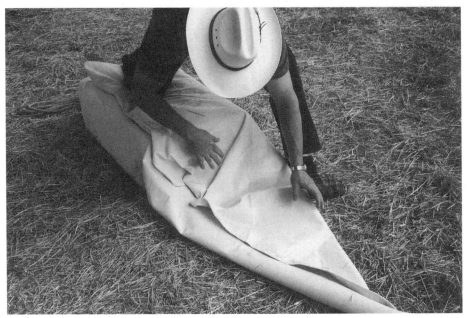

7-4-k

7-4-l

7-4-m

That takes care of the mantie, now let's secure the pack with our cargo rope.

1. Take the cargo rope from your belt or pick it up from where you laid it at the toe of the pack. Undo the rope and while holding the eye splice in your left hand, toss the running end of the rope away from you at about a 45 degree angle, figures 7-5, a & b.

2. Build a loop in the rope large enough to fit over the pack, end to end. Place the loop around the pack, the end of the eye splice should be "facing" you and it should be located at the top front edge of the pack. This step is made easier if you lean backwards with your knees still on the pack, thus lifting the right side off the ground a bit so your rope will easily fit under the pack. Hold the eye splice in your left hand and position it exactly where you want it at the top-front corner. Now pull the loop tight, figures 7-5, c - e. **From this point on you must never allow slack in the rope. Keep it as tight as possible at all times.**

3. Now you need to make three half hitches around the pack. I like to put two half hitches on from the top end, and then turn around and put the third hitch on from the bottom. Some packers like to put on one, then turn around and put on two. This is strictly personal preference and habit, and

has no functional bearing on the quality of the cargoing job. The hitches must be removed from the same end they were put on, however, or you will end up with a knot in your cargo rope. This step will require some practice to master, but once you get the hang of it, the motions are repetitive and they will become very automatic. Review the picture sequence figures 7-5, f - o to visualize the technique of applying the three half hitches. The middle half hitch should be directly in the center of the pack, and the top and bottom hitches should be roughly six to eight inches from each end. The top hitch should secure the rain flap.

4. As you secure the bottom half hitch and pull it tight, roll the pack on its side, then bring your cargo rope around the bottom and along the back side of the pack. Roll the pack onto its back and on the rope. Stand the pack up by lifting on the cargo rope and rest the pack on your leg. Again, pull the rope tight and you are ready for the final tie, figures 7-5, p - s.

5. There are countless knots that can be used to tie off the pack. This knot must be secure, but it also must be easily untied when it is time to undo the pack. My preference for this knot is the "basket hitch" tie. This is the very same knot we will use to tie off the pack when we load it on our pack mule. Follow the picture sequence figures 7-5, t – z to see how to tie this knot.

7-5-a

7-5-b

7-5-c

7-5-d

7-5-e

7-5-f

7-5-g

7-5-h

7-5-i

7-5-j

7-5-k

7-5-l

7-5-m

7-5-n

7-5-o

7-5-p

7-5-q

7-5-r

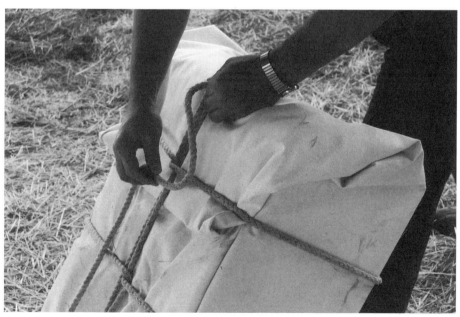

7-5-s

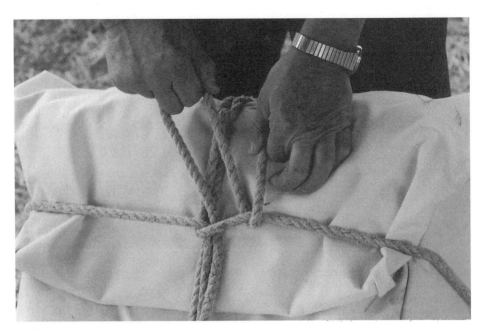

7-5-t

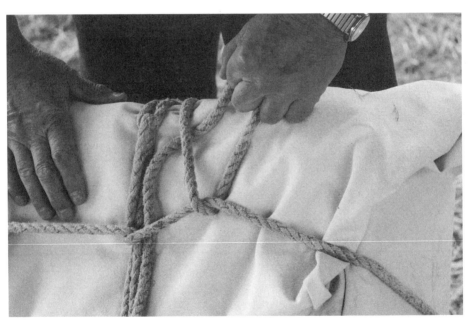

7-5-u

7-5-v

7-5-w

7-5-x

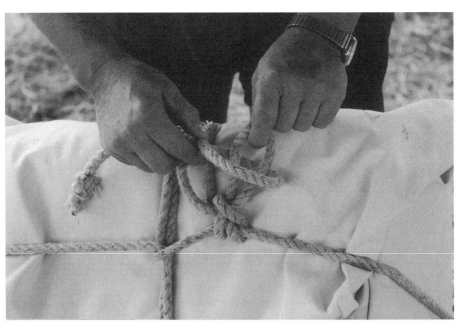

7-5-y

7-5-z

To undo the pack, simply pull on the basket hitch knot and follow the rope back around the pack. Slip the half hitches off the pack from the same end they were put on, pull on the eye splice to loosen the loop, and remove the loop from the pack. At this point, **do not let go of the cargo rope!** While the cargo rope is in hand it is most efficient to "put it up" at this time. Simply make an eighteen inch loop, then coil the rope like a lariat from your left hand to your right hand. Transfer the coiled rope to your left hand, now take the bottom of the first loop and wrap it around the coil one time and pass the end of the loop from your right hand to the fingers of your left hand and pull the loop through the coil in the rope, see figures 7-6, a - i.

7-6-a

7-6-b

7-6-c

7-6-d

7-6-e

7-6-f

7-6-g

7-6-h

7-6-i

CHAPTER EIGHT

DECKER HITCHES

Another advantage of Decker Style Packing is that the basic hitches are quite simple, they are repetitive (once you master them, both sides on every pack animal is tied the same), and they work. Also, adjustments to achieve proper balance can be accomplished in seconds. With traditional Decker Style Packing, most loads are cargoed and tied on with the Basket Hitch. This hitch will likely be used over 90 percent of the time. Other useful hitches are the Barrel Hitch, and what I call the Decker Diamond. In this Chapter I will fully illustrate these three basic hitches, as well as, two tie-down hitches, and I will illustrate how to "put up" the sling rope when the saddle is empty and when loaded. Additionally, I will discuss the use of panniers and top packs and other special bunks, bags and useful equipment.

The Basket Hitch
Take the sling rope down from the rear bow of the saddle and configure the rope as illustrated in figure 8-1, a. The sling rope is tied off on the front bow, a loop big enough to accommodate the side-pack is formed, and the running end of the rope is passed through the rear bow from the back to the front. This rope is then fed under the loop, and the excess sling rope is looped and laid on the back of the mule (lay it on the neck on the right side of the mule). Laying the excess rope up on the back and neck of the mule will keep the rope cleaner and you or the mule will not become entangled in it should the mule move to the side.

Now place the side-pack on the mule so the top-rear edge of the pack is in the center of the mule's back, figure 8-1, b. (If you are loading by yourself, you may need to place the first pack up higher and tie it down

8-1-a, Basket Hitch

8-1-b, Basket Hitch

so the load will not roll while you prepare to hang the other side. If you do this, now simply hang the off side, then go back and adjust the first side down into proper position. Now adjust the right side to achieve proper position and balance.)

Pull the loop in the sling rope under the side-pack and onto the front side of the pack. As you do this you must support the pack with your arms or your side, or probably a combination of both. Now pull slack out of the sling rope by pulling with your right hand on the running end of the rope from the bottom of the pack as in figure 8-1, c. The horizontal portion of the sling rope (see left hand in figure 8-1, c) should be at a point on the pack that is about 1/3 of the distance down from the top of the pack. Pull the pack tight against the bows of the saddle, figure 8-1, d, and without allowing any slack in the sling rope, wrap the rope around the bottom of the pack and up the front side to where it can be tied off on the horizontal part of the sling rope, figure 8-1, e. The Basket Hitch Tie is fully illustrated in Chapter Nine, see figures 9-3, a - f.

8-1-c, Basket Hitch

8-1-d, Basket Hitch

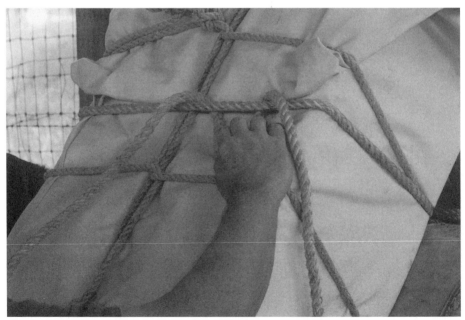

8-1-e, Basket Hitch

The Barrel Hitch

The barrel hitch is an excellent way to pack round and/or long objects such as barrels, rounds of firewood, hind quarters of elk, or post and pole material. It too is a rather simple hitch, however, attention to specific sling rope layout is important as you begin. Follow this sequence to tie the barrel hitch:

Take the sling rope down so it is attached only to the front bow, see figure 8-2, a.

1. Form a loop ahead of the front bow big enough to accommodate the side-pack, figure 8-2, b.

2. Pass a loop through the rear bow from front to back, also making this loop big enough to fit the load. Pay special attention that the running end of the rope is <u>on top</u> as it passes back through the rear bow. This is crucial so that a pinch does not occur as the rope is being tightened around the load, figure 8-2, c.

3. Drape the running end down the side between the two bows and loop the excess rope in the quarter strap so it is up off the ground and out of the way, figure 8-2, d. Set the rope up in similar fashion on the off side and you are ready to load. Before you place the load, however, look to see which ropes to pull to tighten each loop. You must pull on the front side of the rear loop to tighten the front loop, and pull on the running end of the rope to tighten the rear loop.

4. Place the load on the saddle with the front end of the pack slightly higher than the rear and place the front loop around the pack so the rope will tighten from bottom to top. Pull on the front side of the rear loop to tighten the front loop, figures 8-2, e & f.

5. Position the rear loop over the load and tighten by pulling on the running end of the rope, figures 8-2, g & h.

6. Pass the running end up and over the top of the load and loop it completely around the rope between the two bows, pulling it as tight as possible, figures 8-2, i & j.

7. Pull the running end down and pass it through the small ring in your pack cinch, pull it tight, and tie off on the center of the pack with a clove hitch around the cargo rope of the side-pack, figures 8-2, k - n. Repeat the process on the other side.

8-2-a, Barrel Hitch

8-2-b, Barrel Hitch

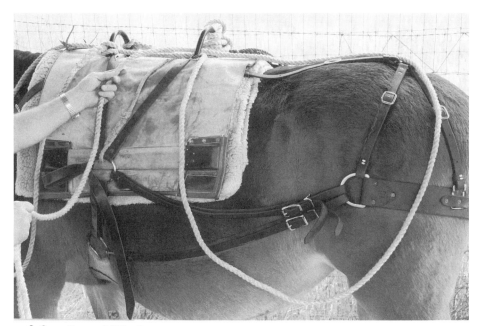

8-2-c, Barrel Hitch

8-2-d, Barrel Hitch

8-2-e, Barrel Hitch

8-2-f, Barrel Hitch

8-2-g, Barrel Hitch

8-2-h, Barrel Hitch

8-2-i, Barrel Hitch

8-2-j, Barrel Hitch

8-2-k, Barrel Hitch

8-2-l, Barrel Hitch

8-2-m, Barrel Hitch

8-2-n, Barrel Hitch

The barrel hitch may not be used very often, but at times, with certain types of loads, it can be more useful and functional than the basket hitch. It is well worth mastering the barrel hitch!

The Decker Diamond

A third hitch I find useful at times is one I call the Decker Diamond. This hitch is used when packing panniers on a Decker and when a top pack is needed. The advantage of the Decker Diamond is that the top pack can be tied on with just the existing sling ropes on the saddle, no additional "lash cinch" is required as on a Sawbuck Saddle. The second advantage of this hitch is that it pulls the panniers up and off of the pack animal's rib cage allowing the animal to breathe freely and taking possible pressure points off the rib cage. Follow these simple steps to tie the Decker Diamond:

1. Start by setting the sling ropes up in a typical basket hitch configuration and then hang your panniers. Either soft or hard sided panniers will work for this hitch, see figure 8-3, a.

2. Load the top pack and check for proper balance. Pull the basket loop of the sling rope under and around the pannier and take this loop all the way up and over the top pack, figures 8-3, b & c.

3. Pull on the running end of the sling rope from the bottom of the pannier to secure the top pack in the basket loop, figure 8-3, d.

4. While maintaining tension on the sling rope, bring the rope up the face of the pannier and tie it off with a standard basket hitch tie. When this tie is pulled tight it will make a "V" in the horizontal sling rope, see figures, 8-3, e - g.

5. Repeat the sequence on the off side and from the top there will be the appearance of a diamond shape in the sling ropes, thus the name Decker Diamond, figure 8-3, h.

8-3-a, Decker Diamond

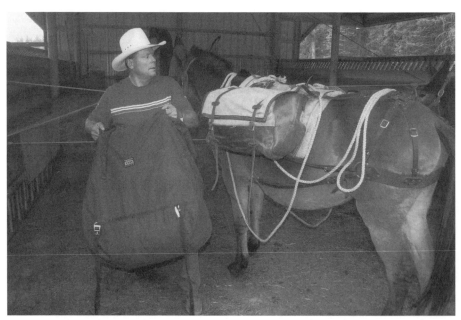

8-3-b, Decker Diamond

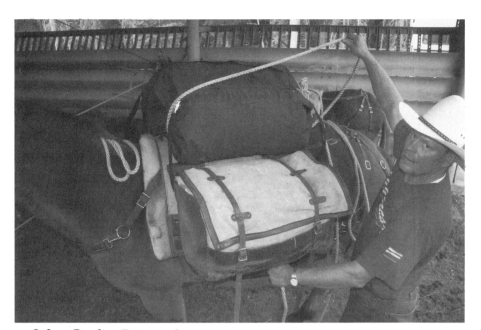

8-3-c, Decker Diamond

8-3-d, Decker Diamond

8-3-e, Decker Diamond

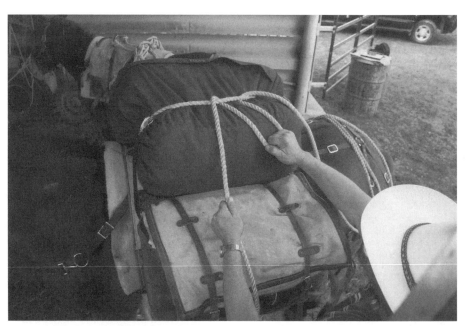

8-3-f, Decker Diamond

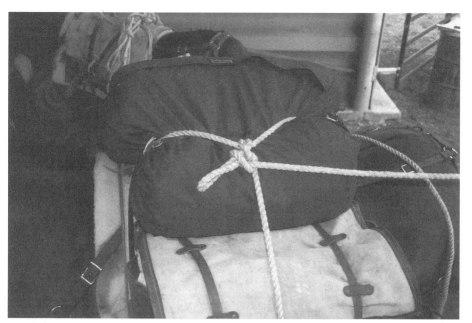

8-3-g, Decker Diamond

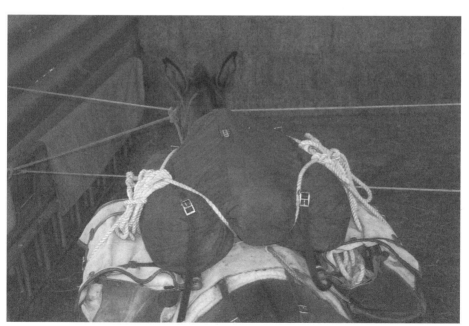

8-3-h, Decker Diamond

Tying Loads Down

Traditional Decker Style Packing calls for cargoed side-packs that are tied on with a basket hitch and allowed to "swing" free at the bottom. There are times, however, when it is advantageous to tie the side-packs down. When traveling cross-country in steep rough terrain it may be advantages to tie down. Also, small side-packs or very light side-packs will have a tendency to bounce and sometimes work free of the basket hitch, and odd shaped, slick, packs such as propane bottles can slip free of the basket hitch. In these situations it is a good idea to tie the load down, however, tying down should be the exception and not the rule. Some packers tie all loads down which is inefficient, and it defeats the "swing free" principle of the Decker Saddle.

Two hitches that work very well for tying a side-pack down are the "Crows-Foot" and the "Christensen Hitch". Both of these hitches utilize the loop from the basket hitch tie and the running end of the sling rope, as well as, the small ring in the pack cinch to accomplish the tie down. The main difference in the two hitches is that the Crows-Foot pulls the side-pack horizontally into the rib cage of the pack animal, figure 8-6, and the Christensen hitch ties the pack vertically so less strain is placed on the rib area, figure 8-7.

My preference for a tie down is the Christensen Hitch. The hitch got its name from a long-time Forest Service Packer named John Christensen of Huson, Montana. John first showed this hitch to several of his packing colleagues over twenty years ago. These two hitches are tied as follows:

The Crows-Foot

1. Tie the side pack in place with the standard basket hitch tie, except do not place the final half-hitch over the loop, figure 8-4, a.

2. Pull the loop out and make it big enough so it fits completely around the side-pack, figures 8-4, b & c.

3. Pull the bottom of the loop through the small ring in the pack cinch, see figure 8-4, d.

4. Feed the running end of the sling rope through the loop and snug tight, figures 8-4, e & f.

5. Complete the tie down by tying off with the basket hitch tie, figure 8-4, g.

8-4-a, Crows-Foot

8-4-b, Crows-Foot

8-4-c, Crows-Foot

8-4-d, Crows-Foot

8-4-e, Crows-Foot

8-4-f, Crows-Foot

8-4-g, Crows-Foot

The Christensen Hitch

1.As with the Crows-foot, tie the side-pack in place with the standard basket hitch and basket hitch tie, leaving the final half-hitch off the loop, see figure 8-5, a.

2. Pull the loop out and pass it around just one side of the pack, then down through the small cinch ring, figures 8-5, b & c.

3. Pass the running end of the sling rope through the loop from the other side of the pack and snug tight, figures 8-5, d & e. Note that the safest place to stand while snugging and tying the load is in the safe zone in front of the pack, not at the rear of the pack. The initial loop should pass to the right side of the pack when tying down the left side-pack and the loop should be placed initially to the left side on the right side-pack.

4. Tie off with a standard basket hitch tie, figure 8-5, f.

8-5-a, Christensen Hitch

8-5-b, Christensen Hitch

8-5-c, Christensen Hitch

8-5-d, Christensen Hitch

8-5-e, Christensen Hitch

8-5-f, Christensen Hitch

8-6 – The Crows-Foot pulls the side-pack horizontally into the ribcage of the pack animal.

8-7 – The Christensen Hitch ties the pack vertically so less strain is placed on the rib area.

Putting Up the Sling Ropes

It might seem that something as simple as tying the excess rope back onto the saddle when either empty or loaded would not be a big deal. It is, however, a rather critical step in the packing process. Improperly put up ropes can lead to dragging ropes which can spook your mules, or it can lead to a lot of inefficiency if you must try to undo a different lash-up each time you pack a saddle. Sling ropes should be put up in a very systematic and repetitive fashion, and they must be tied so there is no possibility of them coming undone.

As with so many facets of the packing profession, there is more than one way to get the job done. One common method of putting up ropes on an empty saddle is to simply make long loops back and forth through the rear bow of the saddle. The loops should extend to two or three inches below the bottom of the half-breed. The series of loops is then tied off with an overhand knot. Each side is put up separately, but both sides are put up on the rear bow.

A second method, and the way I have learned to put up sling ropes, is illustrated in the following written series and photographs. This method of putting up sling ropes is "fail safe" in regard to the rope coming loose unexpectedly, and once you master the technique, it is very fast and efficient. Each sling rope is put up independently, but both are put up on the rear bows.

1. Once the side-pack is removed, you are left with the basket hitch configuration, figure 8-8, a.

2. Pull the loop of the basket hitch across from the front bow to the rear bow and over the running end of the sling rope, figure 8-8, b. Shorten the loop to about two or three inches below the half-breed, figure 8-8, c.

3. Flip a small loop over the rear bow with the running end of the sling rope, then pull a loop through the rear bow from right to left, see figures 8-8, d & e. Pull this loop down to where it is about one inch shorter than the previous loop, figure 8-8, f.

4. Pull the running end to the left across the loops, then flip another small loop and pull a loop through the rear bow as before, figures 8-8, g - i. Repeat this step until all but two to three feet of the sling rope is up.

5. Now simply tie off the loops with an <u>overhand</u> knot, figures 8-8, j & k. Repeat the process on the other side and your ropes are up.

8-8-a, Putting Up Sling Ropes (unloaded)

8-8-b, Putting Up Sling Ropes (unloaded)

8-8-c, Putting Up Sling Ropes (unloaded)

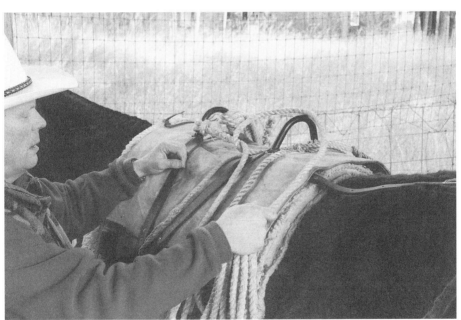

8-8-d, Putting Up Sling Ropes (unloaded)

8-8-e, Putting Up Sling Ropes (unloaded)

8-8-f, Putting Up Sling Ropes (unloaded)

8-8-g, Putting Up Sling Ropes (unloaded)

8-8-h, Putting Up Sling Ropes (unloaded)

8-8-i, Putting Up Sling Ropes (unloaded)

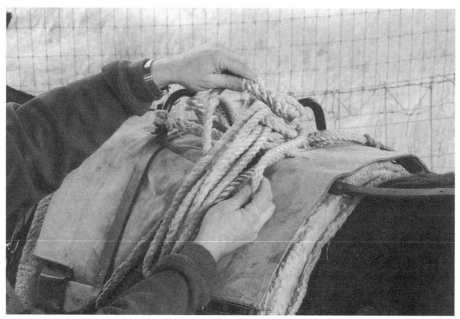

8-8-j, Putting Up Sling Ropes (unloaded)

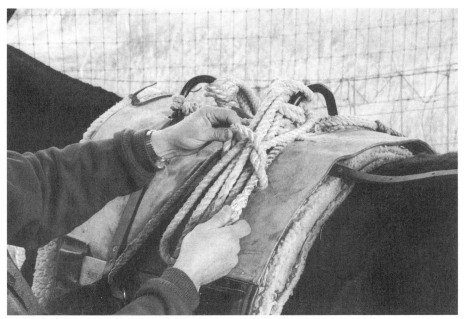

8-8-k, Putting Up Sling Ropes (unloaded)

Putting up excess sling rope on a loaded saddle also requires deliberate consideration. Some packers simply tie the excess onto the side-pack so it is up and out of the way. The problem with tying to the side-pack is that if you need to make an adjustment you must always remove this slack to make the adjustment, and then you must tie it back on again. Also, when you unload the pack you must take the sling rope down where it can end up on the ground, or you or your mule can get tangled in it. The method I prefer for putting up the sling rope on a loaded saddle is as follows:

1. Once the load is hung and the basket hitch tie is complete, take the excess sling rope, and working to your right, make loops around the bow. From the left side of the pack mule put the rope up on the back bow, and from the right, put it on the front bow. (This assumes you are right handed) See figures 8-9, a & b.

2. Make loops until there is about two feet of rope remaining, then tie an overhand knot around the loops, figure 8-9, c.

3. Now when you wish to make a load adjustment, or when you wish to remove the load, **do not take the excess rope off of the bows!** Simply remove the basket hitch tie, adjust the load, now re-tie the basket

hitch tie. If the load is being removed, leave the excess tied to the bows until the mule is moved away from your campsite, figure 8-9, d. After a long trip, mules have a natural tendency to urinate or defecate soon after they stop. If this is in your campsite it can be an unpleasant situation. Leaving the ropes tied up allows you to move the mule immediately out of camp once they are unloaded. This reduces the risk of a deposit in your campsite.

8-9-a, Putting Up Sling Ropes (loaded)

8-9-b, Putting Up Sling Ropes (loaded)

8-9-c, Putting Up Sling Ropes (loaded)

8-9-d, Putting Up Sling Ropes (loaded)

Panniers and Top Packs

Traditional Decker Style Packing is based on cargoed side-packs that are slung from the saddle and allowed to swing free at the bottom. The construction of the Decker Pack Saddle, however, also makes it an excellent saddle for accommodating panniers and a top pack. The protective half-breed and wooden pack boards along with the steel bows makes this saddle very suitable for carrying panniers or pack boxes and a top pack. Disadvantages of panniers are the inability to consistently optimize weight, and the inability to pack larger, awkward loads. Care must be taken that panniers or pack boxes are not hung too low which can put undo pressure on the rib cage and make the load awkward for the animal to carry. Pack boxes and a top pack are convenient, even to the point of commercially available systems such as the Ralide-West "Not-A-Knot Pack System" which requires no ropes or knots, just buckles and snaps, see figure 8-10.

8-10 – Not-A-Knot System

Bear Resistant Pack Boxes

When traveling in bear country it is often a requirement that you keep food and other attractants unavailable to bears. This can be accomplished by either hanging your food (this is not always as simple as it sounds), or you can use an approved bear resistant container. Many styles of bear resistant boxes are commercially available, in both Decker and pack box style, figure 8-11. Some models have stoves built into them, and there are even "cooler" models. These boxes are an excellent option if you are planning a trip in bear country.

8-11 – Bear Resistant Containers

Specialized Pack Equipment

Not everyone would have occasion to use, or have a need for specialized equipment such as "lumber bunks" or "gravel bags". However, if you have an interest in contract packing, or possibly you are involved with a volunteer project along with a local horse club, i.e., Back Country Horsemen, then these two pieces of equipment could be of interest to you.

Gravel bags, figure 8-12, attach directly to the bows of the saddle with a piece of chain. A metal ring on top holds the bag open so that gravel, dirt, rocks, etc, can be placed in the bag. The bag is open on the bottom, but the bottom is folded up and secured with a basket hitch tie for loading. When it is time to dump, simply pull the knot and let the material fall to the ground. Be sure to use gentle stock, or train stock under controlled conditions before heading to a project.

Lumber bunks are used for hauling long material, see figure 8-13. Material that is four feet to twelve feet long can be hauled on a single mule by using lumber bunks. These bunks protect the animal by holding the load away so it cannot rub the animal, and they make loading safer and easier for the packer. The bunks attach to the front bow and the cinch, and they hang on the side of the pack animal. A piece of wood holds the bunk out from the animal's side, and a steel "J" hook extends out to cradle the load. The load is secured in the bunk with the sling rope and a second rope that is attached to the lumber bunk.

8-12 – Gravel Bags

8-13 – Lumber Bunks

Useful Equipment

Two pieces of equipment I find very useful are scrim nosebags and pack scales. Even though nosebags are not specifically a part of the packing sequence, they are used so often that I feel they are worth mentioning. There are numerous types and styles of nosebags available, but the style I prefer is the simple "scrim" bag tied with a light rope. Scrim is a porous, nylon material that allows dust to fall away from the feed and it allows the animal to breathe freely while they eat. The bags are lightweight and not bulky. Mules generally require a larger bag than a horse, figure 8-14, a.

Pack scales are a convenient option, especially when you are just starting into the packing world. Generally, as you gain experience packing, you can develop a "feel" for the weight of your packs, but a handy scale removes the guess work. Some mules require very evenly balanced loads in order for the load to ride properly, and it only makes good sense to weigh the packs if a scale is available. A lightweight portable scale (weights up to 100 pounds) is available that is easily packed, figure 8-14, b, and the heavier 300 pound model, figure 8-14, c, is handy when used at home or at the trailhead.

8-14-a, Nosebags

8-14-b, Pack Scales

8-14-c, Pack Scales

I have purposely kept this "Hitches" chapter as simple and traditional as possible. Other hitches exist (Box Hitch, Diamond Hitch, Salmon River Hitch, etc.) However, I do not find these hitches as humane or as efficient as those described. Virtually anything, within the constraints of weight and bulk, can be packed with the hitches presented. Master these hitches and you can pack anything to any location!

Although I prefer traditional Decker style packing, Decker saddles are very functional with panniers and a top pack.

Ropes, knots and splicing are an integral part of Decker packing.

CHAPTER NINE

ROPES, KNOTS, AND SPLICING

It is important to understand the different ropes, knots, and splices of the Decker system if you wish to be a proficient packer.

In this chapter I present specifications for five ropes: the halter rope, cargo rope, sling rope, pigtail, and the breakaway. I will also illustrate six knots: The common horse tie, a Bowline, the Basket Hitch Tie, the Cargo Tie, the Pigtail Tie and a rope halter tie. I have included sketches of the back-splice and eye-splice, however, you may need additional coaching from someone who knows how to splice. Splicing is difficult to illustrate in sketches or pictures, but it is an important concept to master. Entire books have been written on knots. I will present only those few knots important to Decker Packing.

Ropes

Over the years I have used about every type of rope imaginable and I have developed a very strong bias for a particular brand of rope. With only the exception of using Manila rope for breakaways, my preference in rope is New England Brand, Multi-Line II. This rope is a three-strand composite with a polyester cover and polyoelfin core. For years I have referred to this rope as "three-strand, soft-spun nylon." This actually is incorrect as there is no nylon in this particular rope. The composite stretches very little, it is strong, and it wears very well. It is easy on your hands compared to many other brands of rope, it holds knots well, it does not freeze in cold weather, and it is easy to back-splice and eye-splice.

Halter Rope: ½ inch diameter, cut twelve feet long with eye-splice on one end and back-splice on the other.

Cargo Rope: ⅜ inch diameter, cut 35 feet long with eye-splice on one end and back-splice on the other.

Sling Rope: ½ inch diameter, cut 24 - 28 feet long with eye-splice and back-splice.

Pigtail: ⅜ inch diameter, cut 7 feet long. Find the center of the rope and tie the two sides together about twelve inches from the center point. This can be done with a simple knot, or better yet, use a "Fish Knot". Lay the rope in the middle of the saddle and drape an end to each rigging ring with the loop extending through and beyond the rear bow 8 -12 inches toward the rear of the saddle. Eye splice an end of the Pigtail rope around each rigging ring making sure to keep the Pigtail loop centered on the saddle, but allowing the two sides to "Y" back toward the rear bow. Attach a 1/4 inch Manila breakaway to the Pigtail loop.

Breakaway: ¼ inch to ⅜ inch Manila rope. Breakaways can be made in a loop by splicing or tying the two ends together, or my preference is to cut a rope about 3 feet long and put an eye-splice on each end. Simply place one loop of the breakaway over the Pigtail loop. Now thread the other breakaway loop through the Pigtail loop. Tie the halter rope into this breakaway loop.

Knots
Common Horse Tie:

1. Wrap the halter rope around a solid object and make a "figure 4" as shown in figure 9-1, a.

2. Leaving a loop in the running end of the halter rope (working end is attached to the halter), tie a simple knot around the halter rope, see figures 9-1, b-d.

3. Push the knot up tight against the post or rail, figure 9-1, e.

4. Turn a half-hitch around the loop from the working end of the halter rope, figure 9-1, f. This will keep the knot from getting too tight should the mule pull back and put strain on the halter rope.

9-1-a, Common Horse Tie

9-1-b, Common Horse Tie

9-1-c, Common Horse Tie

9-1-d, Common Horse Tie

9-1-e, Common Horse Tie

9–1-f, Common Horse Tie

Bowline: The Bowline is used whenever a rope is tied around the neck, i.e. when tying up a foot. Once tied, this knot will not tighten when tension is put on the rope, and it can always be untied by simply rolling the looped ends back. There are many ways to tie a Bowline. This is how I do it.

    1. Place rope around the animal's neck and make a "figure 6" in the rope, figure 9-2, a.

    2. Thread the running end of the rope up through the "6", figure 9-2, b.

    3. Wrap the running end around the upper leg of the rope, figure 9-2, c, now pass the running end back down through the "6", figure 9-2, d. Pull the knot tight, figure 9-2, e.

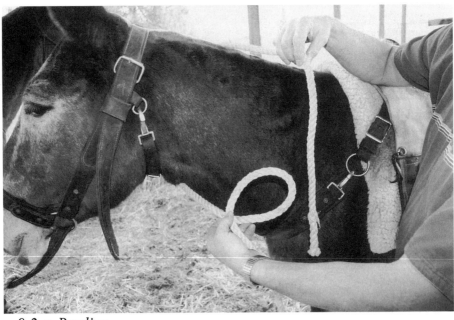

9-2-a, Bowline

9-2-b, Bowline

9-2-c, Bowline

9-2-d, Bowline

9-2-e, Bowline

Basket Hitch Tie: This tie is used to secure cargoed loads to the saddle.

1. After forming the basket around the side-pack with the swing rope, bring the running end of the swing rope up and pass a loop over the top of the horizontal portion of the swing rope, figure 9-3, a.

2. Pass the loop under the vertical portion of the swing rope and pull it tight, figure 9-3, b. This is a step some packers fail to complete. Without it, the knot can come undone and the pack will fall off.

3. Roll the loop up and pinch it with your left thumb and forefinger, see figure 9-3, c.

4. Pull a loop through this loop with the running end of the rope and pull tight, figures 9-3, d & e. (Be sure to pull the loop from above the horizontal swing rope, not from below it.) Now shorten the loop to about 4 inches.

5. Turn a half-hitch around the loop to secure it, figure 9-3, f.

9-3-a, Basket Hitch Tie

9-3-b, Basket Hitch Tie

9-3-c, Basket Hitch Tie

9-3-d, Basket Hitch Tie

9-3-e, Basket Hitch Tie

9-3-f, Basket Hitch Tie

Cargo Tie: I have already illustrated the Cargo Tie I use (see figures 7-5, t - z). It is the very same knot as the Basket Hitch Tie (figures 9-3, a - f).

Another option for a Cargo Tie Knot is as follows:

    1. As you bring the cargo rope over the top of the side-pack to the front side, pass a loop from the running end of the cargo rope under the vertical cargo rope, just below the top half hitch, figures 9-4, a & b.

    2. Roll this loop up and across the vertical ropes and tuck this loop back through the loop just created. This is simply a knot with a loop left in it, figures 9-4, c & d.

    3. Tighten the knot and put a half hitch on it to secure it. Tuck the loose end and the loop under the horizontal half hitch, figures 9-4, e & f.

9-4-a, Cargo Tie

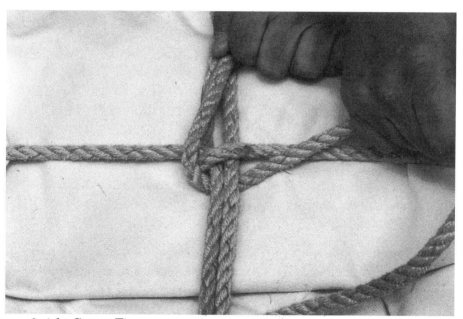

9-4-b, Cargo Tie

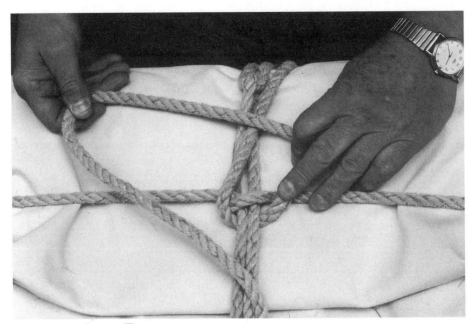

9-4-c, Cargo Tie

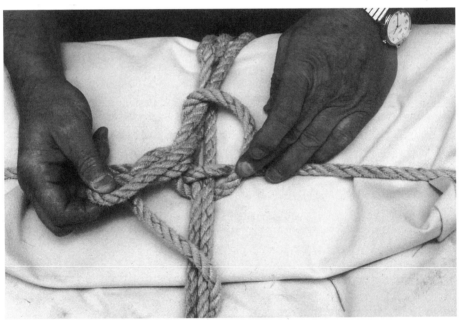

9-4-d, Cargo Tie

9-4-e, Cargo Tie

9-4-f, Cargo Tie

Pigtail Tie: This knot is used to tie mules together in a pack train. It will not pull tight with tension and can always be untied.

1. Loop the halter rope through the break away on the Pigtail Rope, see figure 9-5, a.

2. Gather the loop and the running end of the halter rope together, see figure 9-5, b.

3. Turn a half hitch around the loop and running end, figure 9-5, c.

9-5-a, Pigtail Tie

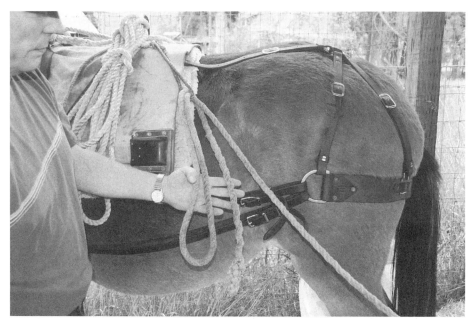

9-5-b, Pigtail Tie

9-5-c, Pigtail Tie

Rope Halter Tie: This tie is shown in figure 9-6, a. Note that the tie is made below the loop and not above it. If you tie above and the horse pulls back, the knot can get so tight that you can't untie it. Also, be sure the loose end is away from the horse's eye. The sequence of tying this knot is shown in figures, 9-6, b – e.

9-6-a, Rope Halter Tie

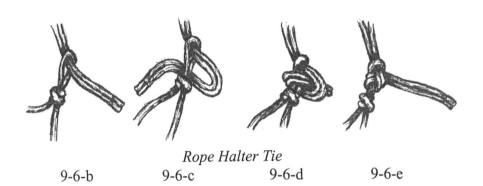

Rope Halter Tie

| 9-6-b | 9-6-c | 9-6-d | 9-6-e |

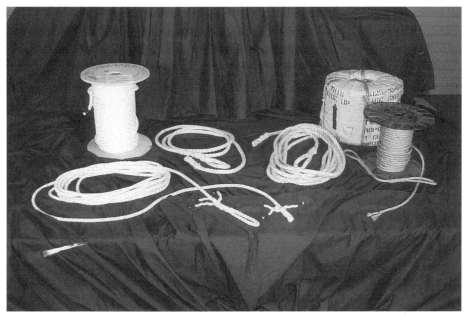

Learning to back-splice is an important facet of packing.

Splicing

Back-Splice: The back-splice is used on the running end of all three-strand ropes to keep them from fraying. Follow this sequence to tie the back-splice:

1. Unbraid the three strands of rope four or five inches from the end, see figure 9-7, a. The rope strands are color coded white, black, and shaded to assist this illustration.

2. Hold the end of the rope vertical and pinch it at the bottom of the unbraided strands so they do not continue to unravel. With the middle strand toward you (shaded strand), take the end of this strand directly away from you and pinch it on the backside of the rope with your pointer finger. Your thumb should be on the front side, see figure 9-7, b.

3. Take the white strand and wrap it around to the rear of the loop you just made with the shaded strand, and pass it between the shaded strand and the black strand, figure 9-7, c. Pinch it with your thumb.

4. Now take the black strand and pass it over the top of the white strand and through the loop made by the shaded strand, figure 9-7, d. Continue to pinch at the bottom of the unbraided strands, now gently pull on each strand to tighten the knot and form a "button" at the end of the rope. This is called a Crown Knot. The three strands will be equal distance apart and will form a symmetrical "Y" shape, figure 9-7, e.

5. Now lay the rope vertical and take any strand (in this case the shaded strand) and pass it over the strand lying next to it (the black strand) and go under the next stand (the shaded strand). Turn the rope 1/3 of a turn away from you and do the same with the next strand (black) passing it over the white strand and under the black strand, figures 9-7, f & g. Repeat this step for the third strand and you will be back to three strands, equal distance apart, forming a symmetrical "Y" shape.

6. Repeat step five a total of three times and your back-splice is complete. Cut off the excess from the three strands and lightly melt the ends with a match or lighter. Roll the completed splice between your hands to make all the strands lay in their proper position, figure 9-7, h.

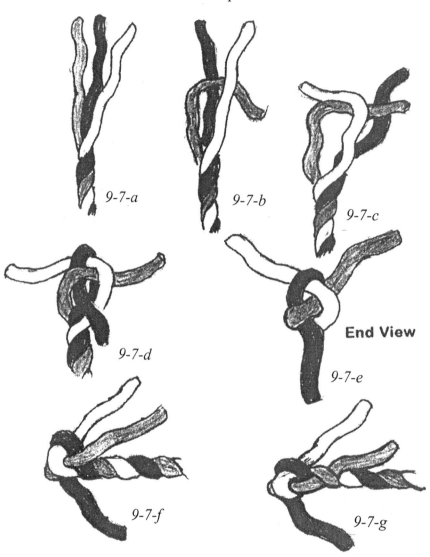

9-7-a

9-7-b

9-7-c

9-7-d

End View

9-7-e

9-7-f

9-7-g

9-7-h

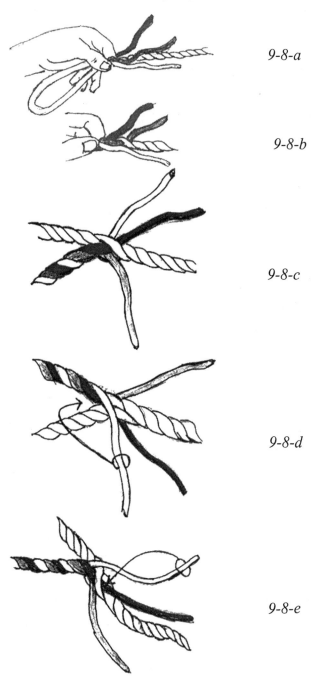

9-8-a

9-8-b

9-8-c

9-8-d

9-8-e

Eye-Splice: The eye-splice is the best way to prepare a rope so you can make a loop in the rope. Follow this sequence to make an eye-splice:

1. Unbraid the three strands of rope four or five inches from the end. Pinch the rope at the bottom of the unbraided strands so they do not continue to unravel. Fold the loop back over itself a distance of about four inches to make a loop, figure 9-8, a. The strands are color coded black, shaded, and white in this illustration.

2. Start with the shaded strand in the middle and toward you, now place the strand over the rope with the middle (shaded) strand on top, the black strand is to the left side and white strand is to the right side.

3. Take the middle strand (shaded) and go under any strand in the rope, figure 9-8, b.

4. Roll the loop 1/3 turn away from you and take the next strand (black) over the strand lying next to it and under the next strand, going in where the last (shaded) strand came out, figure 9-8, c.

5. Rotate the loop 1/3 turn again, at this point I like to pass the third (white) strand back through the loop and turn the loop over, figure 9-8, d. This makes a "natural lay" for the white strand to go over the strand lying next to it and under the next strand, going in where the last strand (black) came out, figure 9-8, e.

6. Repeat back splice steps 5 & 6, two or three times, and the eye-splice is complete.

I realize these splices are not easy to follow but practice will make perfect. It's like riding a bike, once you get it, you likely won't ever forget it. If you have trouble getting it, ask someone who knows how to assist you. It is well worth knowing how to back-splice and eye-splice.

CHAPTER TEN

CARING FOR YOUR TACK

With care, your saddle(s) can give you a lifetime of service. Saddles are not cheap and caring for them properly seems only to make good sense. Also, to keep equipment safe, proper maintenance is essential. Every time a saddle is used it should be checked for worn parts, especially latigos, straps, and ropes. Any worn or deteriorating piece should be replaced immediately. Don't wait for a part to break before it is replaced! Broken equipment while on a pack trip can result in significant inconvenience, or worse, injury to animals or humans. Keep saddles in a safe, functional state of repair at all times.

In addition to being in a good condition, it is important to keep saddles clean and well oiled. This is not "rocket science", but keeping saddles clean and well oiled does require considerable effort and "elbow grease". Also, it is important to use the right products (soaps, oils, conditioners). Remember, leather is like skin, so only use products on leather that you would be willing to put on your own skin.

Aside from keeping your saddles in a good state of repair, proper maintenance of your tack can be looked at as a two or three step process. All tack (riding saddles, pack saddles, bridles, leather halters, etc) should be cleaned and oiled at least annually or semi-annually. Riding saddles and bridles should also be conditioned with a good saddle dressing. It is a good idea to condition pack saddles also, however, depending on the number of saddles you are working with, cleaning and oiling will suffice.

Cleaners are soaps that remove surface dirt and expose the pores of the leather. You should avoid detergents that can pull oils out of the leather. Cleaners should remove old soap buildup and leave a surface clean for oiling and conditioning.

Oils lubricate the leather. Oil needs to penetrate the leather and coat the fibers of the leather. The oil must be light enough so it will penetrate. Heavy oil or oil applied cold will not evenly distribute itself throughout the total thickness of heavy harness leather and will form a gum on the surface. Oil can be applied while the leather is still damp from soaping as the water will act as a vehicle to carry the oil deep into the leather and deter over-oiling of softer parts of the leather. Two light coats will be better than one heavy coat. A common practice when oiling pack saddle parts is "dipping" in a large pan of oil and hanging to drip dry. This is not a recommended practice as it can result in over-oiling. This can cause the leather fibers to separate and eventually weaken the leather. (Although dipping is not recommended, it is probably better than doing nothing.) Apply oils at warm temperatures, between 80 and 90 degrees.

Conditioners provide a finished look to the leather. They fill the grain and allow the edges to be burnished to a smooth finish. They give the leather a rich look and supple feel. Most can be buffed. This finished look is nice on riding saddles and bridles but generally not applied to pack saddles. Conditioners will provide a protective coating that will provide some degree of water repellence, and they can keep the oil from drying out while keeping the leather lubricated.

The process to use to properly care for your saddle is to: (1) clean, (2) lubricate, and (3) condition. The first step in saddle cleaning is to completely disassemble the saddle so all leather parts are exposed for cleaning. **Caution: Pay close attention to how the saddle comes apart so you are able to put it back together properly!**

Clean your saddle with a good quality **glycerin saddle soap**, using a moderate amount of water. This is preferable to liquid soaps. Work up a good lather and clean thoroughly but gently. Excessively dirty areas can be cleaned with Castile or other mild soap. Do not use detergent or soap with additives. Give special attention to areas of the saddle that come in contact with the horse or mule, i.e. breeching and breast collar. A bristle brush or tooth brush works well to remove stubborn caked-on dirt and residue. (Stiff wire brushes are not recommended.)

Next, lubricate the saddle parts with a coat of **PURE neatsfoot** or vegetable oil. Again, two light coats are better than one heavy coat. This may be applied while the leather is still moist so the oil will be drawn into the leather as the moisture evaporates. Pure neatsfoot, vegetable oil, or a mixture of the two, is preferable to "prime neatsfoot" or "neatsfoot compound", which may contain as much as 90 percent mineral oil.

Harness oil is another good oil for pack saddles. This is a combination of pure neatsfoot oil with other oils, and some brands contain a deterrent to rats and mice. Always apply oil at a warm room temperature of about 80 to 90 degrees.

Conditioning with an even application of good quality saddle dressing will give your saddle that finished professional look. Warm air from a hair dryer will soften the dressing and open the pores of the leather to give better penetration, preventing excessive surface buildup.

Caring for your tack is an essential and responsible part of being in the packing business. Take pride in your outfit and keep it maintained. Other packers you meet on the trail may not remember your name, but they will remember the condition of your pack train!

Packing skills allow you to experience beautiful places, even goat country. How many mountain goats can you find?

CHAPTER 11

LEAVE ONLY TRACKS
EQUIPMENT, TECHNIQUES, PRACTICES

Horses and mules are big, heavy animals that have the ability to cause significant damage to the land (soil) and vegetation. I firmly believe, however, if we manage our stock use, impacts can be minimized and held to an acceptable level. Additionally, our stock are not the only culprits when it comes to causing camping or back country travel impacts. We are responsible for being prepared for a back country trip and for our own conduct, as well as the conduct of our stock. This chapter contains recommended techniques, equipment, and practices to help minimize lasting impacts to the land or to other users.

Following is a list of equipment and practices with supporting rationale that can help us be responsible campers and stock handlers. Entire books and videos have been prepared on this topic and this chapter is intended only as a "tickler" to make you aware of available equipment and practices that can help make you a more responsible stock user. Formal training programs are available from several land managing agencies and from organized stock user groups such as Back Country Horsemen of America.

Equipment
Tent

    1. Select a tent to match party size and expected weather conditions

    2. Modern fabrics may be lighter and less bulky than traditional canvas

    3. Internal frames allow for quicker set up and eliminate need to cut trees for poles

Protective Ground Cloth (Textiline)
1. Protects ground from trampling and scuffing
2. Use on tent floors, in kitchen areas, or around camp fires
3. Keeps tent interiors clean and easy to sweep, material is porous and doesn't absorb water

Lightweight Chairs, Cots & Tables
1. Eliminates need to construct furniture from native materials
2. Easy to pack in and pack out

Collapsible, Packable Wood Stove for Heating
1. Pack it in, pack it out
2. Use stove pipe that nests together. Cleaner and more convenient to pack in/pack out
3. Utilize fire blanket under stove to reduce fire hazard

Cook Stove/Lantern
1. Cook on gas – campfires are for "atmosphere"
2. Aluminum propane tanks are lighter than steel
3. Convenient lantern/stove combinations are available
4. Cooking on gas is cleaner, faster, and requires no wood cutting

Campfire
1. Campfires can blacken rocks, sterilize the soil and attract garbage
2. Build a "No Trace" campfire
3. Utilize existing fire rings, don't build new ones
4. Use a "fire blanket" or "fire pan" for no impact

Toilet (pit or latrine style)
1. Use for larger parties or extended lengths of stay
2. Convenient, packable privacy shelters and folding toilets are available
3. Deposit human waste a minimum of 200 feet away from camp, water and trails
4. Bury/cover human waste 6"-8" in mineral soil
5. Consider packing out soiled toilet paper

Saw/Axe
1. Clear obstacles from trails if you are able
2. Riding around obstacles will create unwanted trails

Shovel/Rake
1. Ideally, all evidence of your stay will be disguised and/or rehabilitated before you leave the campsite
2. Shovel and rake allows you to fill holes, scatter manure, and cover disturbed areas easily

Gravity Flow Water Treatment System
1. Provides clean, Giardia-free drinking water
2. Provides a large volume of water in a short time without manual pumping
3. Elaborate piping systems from creek to camp are generally not acceptable

Bear Resistant Food Storage
1. Check to see if this is mandatory in the area where you plan to camp
2. Bear resistant containers or hanging systems may be required
3. Proper equipment and technique is essential

Lightweight equipment that can be packed to any camp is convenient and comfortable, as well as light on the land.

Leave No Weeds
Noxious weeds have a negative impact on recreationists and on wildlife.
Be Aware and Prepare
1. Check stock, tack, gear and clothing for weed seeds
2. Brush animals to remove weed seeds
3. Feed stock certified weed seed free feed several days before, and during your trip
4. Learn to identify common local weeds
Camp and Travel in Weed Free Areas
1. Stay on established roads and trails
2. Avoid traveling through or camping in weed infested areas

Pull and Pack Out Weeds When Possible
1. Pull only species you can identify
2. Pull only tap rooted species such as knapweed, musk thistle and hounds tongue
3. Leave non-seed producing plants or plant parts on site
4. Bag, and pack out seed producing parts
5. Be careful not to spread seeds on the way home!

Noxious Weed Prevention
1. Feed stock certified grain, hay or pellets
2. Use certified feed several days before and during travel in the back country
3. Know how to make sure the feed is certified weed seed free
4. Tags on bales or bags
5. Special twine on bales
6. Use a brush/curry on your animals before and after your trip to remove weed seeds

Stock Containment

Improper stock containment can cause serious damage to the land by trampling/killing vegetation, exposing bare soil to erosion, killing trees, polluting water, spreading noxious weeds, overgrazing vegetation, etc.

Several good methods of stock containment exist. Your own personal preference will likely determine the method(s) you use.

It is essential that your stock is trained and accustomed to whatever method(s) you use <u>before</u> you go into the back country.

Some degree of stock containment will be necessary in most back country camping situations. Generally, the less confined an animal is, the less impact there will be on the land. Equipment and techniques for stock handling exist that can reduce impacts to an acceptable level. It is important to have the right equipment and understand the proper techniques of using this equipment.

Stock Equipment

• **Bell** – Use when loose grazing stock. Be sure bells or loose stock do not annoy other users

• **Hobbles** – Use on loose grazing stock or on a tied animal that insists on pawing.

• **Picket** – Good method to allow natural grazing while still constraining an animal. Move picket frequently to prevent overgrazing in one area.

• **Electric corral** – This method allows grazing by one or several animals and yet provides constraint. Move corral frequently to prevent overgrazing.

• **Highline** – Effective method of securing stock in camp, especially when used together with other methods. It is essential to use proper technique to put up highline and to tie stock.

• **Hitch rail** – Effective restraint method, however requires cutting a tree (pole). Always tie or lash the hitch rail and never use nails. Dismantle when breaking camp.

• **Nylon mesh nosebags** – Allows maximum utilization of grain and manufactured feeds.

• **Nylon mesh mangers** – Provides for complete utilization of hay without waste. Cleanup and restoration of stock holding area is much easier when manger is used.

• **Fly spray** – Flies and other biting insects can cause stock to be more restless thus causing more disturbance to the ground. Fly sprays can limit the restlessness and excessive pawing, dusting, or rolling.

Practices for Parties with Stock

    A. Equipment and Trip Preparation

        1. Use properly trained stock

        2. Carry appropriate equipment

        3. Minimize the number of stock (carry optimum weight on each animal)

    B. Practices When Traveling on Existing Trails

        1. Stock should stay on established trails as much as possible

        2. Remove trail obstacles instead of skirting them

        3. Lead stock on the trail, rather than loose-herd them

        4. Tie stock off trail, on a durable site, when taking a break

    C. Campsite Selection

        1. Avoid places that have already been heavily grazed

    D. Campsite Behavior

        1. Keep stock off campsites as much as possible

        2. Keep lengths of stay at one place short

    E. Watering, Feeding, and Grazing Stock

        1. Water stock downstream from drinking sources on a durable site

        2. Carry an appropriate amount of weed-free supplemental feed

3. Place feed and salt on a tarp or in a feedbag or container
4. Minimize confinement of stock when grazing; move picketed stock frequently

F. Confining Stock
   1. Use existing hitch rails and corrals where available; loose graze if possible
   2. Where confinement is necessary, use high lines, pickets, hobbles, and/or electric fence corrals on durable site away from water
   3. Avoid tying stock to trees, particularly small trees for long periods of time

G. Campfires
   1. Consider packing firewood to your camp. A barrel hitch works great for this purpose.

H. Extended Stay Camping
   1. Consider having someone take your stock out to the trailhead or home, and bring them back when you are ready to break camp.

I. **Cleanup/Rehab**
   1. Renovate pawed-up areas; scatter manure; remove picket pins and excess feed and salt. This is the most important step of all the recommended practices unfortunately, it is often the step that is forgotten!

We are fortunate to have millions of acres of private and public land available to us for basically unrestricted stock use. If we are to continue this privilege, it is essential we educate ourselves in proper back country travel practices and, at all times, practice what we have learned. LEAVE ONLY TRACKS – TAKE ONLY MEMORIES.

CHAPTER TWELVE

OTHER USEFUL INFORMATION

Feeding

What you feed your stock may vary depending on what part of the country you are in, so I will not be real specific on types of feed to use. In general, horses are grass eaters and they survive just fine on good grass pasture, on native grasses in back country settings, or on grass hay. It is quite common to feed an alfalfa/grass mix hay to horses and mules as the alfalfa increases production of the hay crop. Feeding straight alfalfa is not recommended, or at least must be fed with caution, as this can be too rich of a feed for your horse and can result in colic or founder, both serious health problems. Never allow horses or mules to feed in growing alfalfa fields and never feed grass clippings. This is an open invitation to serious health problems! Also, use extreme caution in the spring when converting from a winter feeding situation to green grass. Accustom your stock to this change-over slowly to avoid problems with colic and founder. Certain animals may be more susceptible to colic and founder than others, and horses are generally more susceptible than mules.

In back country packing situations we are faced with using native feed, packing 100 percent supplemental feed, or using a combination of native and supplemental feed. Many states or land managing agencies now require Certified Weed Seed Free Feed to prevent the spread of noxious weeds. Be sure to check on this requirement before traveling to any back country area.

Supplemental feeds come in the form of hay bales, hay cubes, compressed hay, complete feed pellets, various sweet feeds and grain. Working stock should receive twenty five pounds, or the equivalent of twenty-five pounds, of feed each day. When feeding hay, stock should receive about twenty-five pounds of hay and a two pound coffee can of grain each working day. I normally do not feed grain on days when the stock is not working. When using hay cubes, compressed hay, or pellets, the ration can be reduced according to the manufacturer's recommendation. Accustom your stock to this type of feed at home before heading to the back country. It is important to note that stock need to feel full in order to be comfortable. Feeding straight compressed type feeds can result in restless animals that still feel hungry, even though they have received a complete ration of nutrients. Allowing the stock to graze a while or feeding a portion of hay along with the compressed feed is a good feeding alternative.

Shoeing

Good foot care is a responsible part of owning horses and mules. Horses should always be shod for any back country outing and I highly recommend that mules are also shod. Mules have straighter walled, harder feet than horses, and depending on the amount of use and terrain in which you will travel, mules sometimes can get by without shoes. I strongly recommend, however, that you always shoe your mules.

Stock will need to be shod every seven or eight weeks during the working season, and they should be trimmed on a regular basis when not in use. They should have shoes pulled and be trimmed before going onto winter pasture. Good shoeing practices and technique can prevent and/or correct lameness or foot problems, and conversely, neglect or poor farrier service can cause problems. A lame horse is a liability and not an asset to your packing program!

Vaccinations and Worming

Like shoeing and proper feeding, a consistent vaccination and worming program is a responsible part of stock ownership. Unfortunately, the cost associated with this essential maintenance sometimes creates a barrier to getting it done. Consult your local veterinarian to determine the appropriate vaccinations to give your stock. The standard would be a 4-way or 5-way vaccination to cover Eastern & Western Sleeping Sickness, Tetanus, Flu, and Rhino. Other typical vaccinations depending on your location are Strangles and West Nile Virus, and to a lesser extent, Rabies, Viral Arteritis, Venezuelan Sleeping

Sickness, and protection against Endotoxins. Again, consult your local veterinarian for recommended vaccinations.

A consistent de-worming program is essential to good stock maintenance. As a minimum, medication should be administered in the fall before going on winter range, and in the spring as your packing season begins. Medication could be necessary as often as every two or three months depending on local and ground conditions. Again, consult your local veterinarian. No worming product is superior over all others, therefore rotating the type of wormer administered is recommended. Many wormers have the same active ingredients, so you can't just rotate brand names. An Ivermectin product should be included in your worming program because of its ability to kill migrating parasites and bots. The two biggest failures of paste worming are underestimating your horse's weight, and administering the wormer when your horse has a mouth full of food.

Dental Care

Horses and mules can be subject to many of the same dental problems as humans. Obviously, dental abnormalities can affect the ability of the animal to eat properly, affecting overall health. Tooth abscesses, loose teeth, teeth that need to be pulled, etc, are dental problems that most often will need to be attended to by your veterinarian. Another common problem in all equine is molars that wear irregularly and develop sharp edges. This results in the animal not being able to chew and eat properly. If this occurs a procedure called "floating" is necessary. A tool called a float, basically a rasp with a long handle, is used to smooth the edges allowing the teeth to come together so the animal can chew correctly. Check for dental irregularities if you notice signs of not eating properly. A good time to check teeth is while administering worm medicine.

Stock First Aid

As stated at the on-set, this is not a first aid manual. I believe, however, it is only prudent in any stock program to have a basic first aid kit available and have a basic understanding of first aid procedures. Following is a list of items to include in a basic first aid kit. You should add to this list depending on available space and your ability to apply first aid. (Consult with your local veterinarian for their recommendation) Also listed are common health problems, their symptoms, and recommended first aid procedures.

First Aid Kit (Minimum Requirements)

Bandage Scissors	Saline or Eye Wash
Furacin Ointment	Sterile Gauze Sponges
Telfa Pads	Betadine Scrub
Roll Gauze	Betadine Solution
Elasticon 3"	Instant Ice Pack
Antibiotic Eye Ointment	Bute Paste

Possible Additional Items

Furacin Spray	Penicillin
Leg Cottons, Quilts, etc	DS Bactrim Pills
Thermometer	Dipyrone
Stethoscope	Needles, Syringes
Vet Wrap	Forceps

Store in a durable, water and dust-proof container, and remember that some products may have expiration dates.

Wounds
1. Control profuse bleeding – use direst pressure.
2. Trim hair from wound edges, remove any debris.
3. Clean wound with sterile sponges & Betadine scrub. Rinse with saline. Can use Betadine solution in water as a rinse solution.
4. Apply Furacin ointment.
5. Bandage – when necessary – almost all lower leg wounds. Dry the leg – bandages don't stick to wet hair. Use Telfa pads, gauze-Elasticon, or leg cotton with vet wrap depending on nature of wound. Wounds below the knee are serious because it is all bone and tendons. Muscle wounds look bad, but they usually can be repaired.
6. Suturing should be left to your Veterinarian – ideally within 6 – 8 hours.
7. See your Veterinarian for tetanus, antibiotics, further care.

Rope Burns/Saddle Sores
1. Clean area as directed in steps 2 & 3 above.
2. Apply Furacin ointment, or Panalog if available.
3. Administer Bute paste (2 grams/1000 lbs.) to lesson swelling and pain.

Eye Injury
1. Flush with saline or eye wash to remove debris.
2. Apply antibiotic ointment 3 - 4 times daily.
3. Seek immediate veterinary care.

Colic
1. Difficult to treat in the field – often requires veterinary care.
2. Walking the horse may help – don't walk him to death!
3. Dipyrone 20cc IM/1000 lbs. may help. Banamine is also good.

Tying Up
1. Will see sweating, reluctance to move, muscles over the hind end may be hard.
2. Remove all tack. Don't encourage the horse to move. Drape with a blanket.
3. Administer Bute paste 2 -3 grams/1000 lbs.
4. Seek veterinary care.

Normal Values in Horses: Rectal temperature 98 – 101 degrees F
- Heart rate 30 – 40 beats per minute
- Respiratory rate 10 – 16 breaths per minute

Estimating Weight of Horses

Knowing the approximate weight of your horse or mule is important when administering medications or when determining how much they can carry (20 percent of their body weight). Obviously the most accurate measurement would be to weigh them on a scale. Another method is to use a "weight tape" which is a specially calibrated measuring tape based on the length of the animal's heart girth. A third method which can be done mathematically is to measure the animal's heart girth and their body length from the chest to the haunch. To calculate total weight, multiply the heart girth measurement by itself, then by the body length, and then divide that total by 330. (Heart girth X heart girth X body length divided by 330 = total body weight)

Brand and Health Inspections

Brand inspections and health inspections are necessary evils that stockmen must deal with, but we should all realize that rules and regulations regarding these inspections are in place to protect the livestock industry. In general, brand inspections are designed to prevent livestock theft, and health inspections help prevent the spread of contagious diseases. The requirements for brand and health inspections can vary from state to state, so if you are planning a trip across state lines, or even across county lines, it is well worth understanding the requirements. Your local brand inspector and your local veterinarian should be able to advise you on the necessary inspections and tests. Failure to comply can cost you a bunch of money in fines, as well as, considerable inconvenience and embarrassment.

Most states will require a current "annual" or "lifetime" **Brand Inspection** and a **Health Certificate** which can be good for 30 days or six months depending on the type you request. This certificate will also include a **Coggins Certificate** which is a test designed to screen for Equine Infectious Anemia. Some states require an **Import Permit** to return back to your home state which is issued by the State Brand Office. You can apply for an Annual Import Permit, or your veterinarian will get an import number as part of the Health Inspection.

CHAPTER THIRTEEN

MEMORIES THAT LAST FOREVER

The intent of this manual has been to instruct you in the art of packing, specifically, packing in a safe-efficient, manner, in the Decker Packing Style. Hopefully, this goal has/will be met. Practice, trail miles, and wet saddle pads will make this activity second nature to you and your stock. Now it's time for you to take your **Mules**, into the **Mountains**, and create your own everlasting **Memories**! *I WISH YOU WELL!*

This is the first elk I ever packed. It scores 364 net. I only had one packhorse (Bandy), but luckily Ken Miller was with me and we were only one-half of a mile from the truck.

Tim Mueller of Coeur d'Alene, Idaho, riding Buckshot and packing hay to camp in traditional Decker Style.

The best short string I ever had! I'm riding Bear and pulling Tess, Willy, Sue Ellen, and Zipper. A successful hunt!

This is my good friend Roger Inghram. A great photographer, excellent help anywhere-anytime, and good company on the trail!

Rand Herzberg of Red Lodge, Montana. Packing with panniers and a top pack and using a "Decker Diamond".

Tim Resch, Estes Park Outfitters, Estes Park, Colorado. Packing a client's bull and "making a living".

Another good hunt (328 net bull). I had to pack this one eight miles. Note that elk is packed in halves, split lengthwise with hair side down, legs to the rear, tied with a Basket Hitch.

Good friends, good stock, successful hunts, beautiful country! What more could one ask for.

HAPPY TRAILS

LISTING OF BOOKS

Additional copies of **THE PACKER'S FIELD MANUAL** and many other of Stoneydale Press' books on outdoor recreation, big game hunting, or historical reminisces centered around the Northern Rocky Mountain region, are available at many book stores and sporting goods stores, or direct from Stoneydale Press. If you'd like more information, you can contact us by calling a Toll Free Number, **1-800-735-7006**, by writing the address at the bottom of the page, or contacting us on the Web at www.stoneydale.com. Here's a partial listing of some of the books that are available. Call or write for our catalog.

Books By Howard Copenhaver

Copenhaver Country, By Howard Copenhaver, the latest collection of humorous stories. Contains rich humor and studied observations of a land Howard loves and the people he met along the way in a lifetime spent in the wilds. 160 pages, many photographs. Hardcover or softcover editions.

They Left Their Tracks, By Howard Copenhaver, Recollections of Sixty Years as a Wilderness Outfitter, 192 pages, clothbound or softcover editions (One of our all-time most popular books.) Hardcover or softcover editions.

More Tracks, By Howard Copenhaver, 78 Years of Mountains, People & Happiness, 180 pages, clothbound or softcover editions

Mule Tracks: The Last of The Story, By Howard Copenhaver. A rich book filled with wit and tender insights into a life lived as an outfitter and famed storyteller in the wilds of Montana, including many stories about his beloved mules. 176 pages, hardcover or softcover editions.

Historical Reminisces

Indian Trails & Grizzly Tales, By Bud Cheff Sr. Stories out of the Bob Marshall Wilderness by one of Montana's most famous long-time wilderness hunting outfitters. 212 pages, available in clothbound and softcover editions.

70,000 Miles Horseback In The Wilds of Idaho, By Don Habel. Don Habel worked as an outfitter in the Idaho wilderness for more than forty years and has put together a wonderfully detailed and sensitive, as well as occasionally humorous, reminisce of his adventures in the wilds. 180 pages, softcover.

The Potts' Factor Versus Murphy's Law, By Stan Potts. Life story of famous Idaho outfitter Stan Potts, lots of photographs. 192 pages.

Mules & Mountains, By Margie E. Hahn, the story of Walt Hahn, Forest Service Packer, 164 pages, clothbound or softcover editions.

Hunting Books

Solving Elk Hunting Problems, By Mike Lapinski. Hunters today have to constantly solve problems of working elk in close, given the increase in pressure on the elk these days. This is the best information on how to hunt elk today by a recognized expert. 192 pages, many photographs, hardcover or softcover.

High Pressure Elk Hunting, By Mike Lapinski. *The best book available on hunting elk that have become educated to the presence of more hunters working them. Lots of info on hunting these elk.192 pages, many photographs, hardcover or softcover.*

Bugling for Elk, By Dwight Schuh, *the bible on hunting early-season elk. A recognized classic, 164 pages, softcover edition only.*

The Woodsman And His Hatchet, By Bud Cheff. *Subtitled "Eighty Years on Wilderness Survival, " this book gives you practical, common sense advice on survival under emergency conditions in the wilderness. Softcover.*

Memoirs of An Idaho Elk Hunter, By Jens Andersen. *This big book captures the vitality and romance of a lifetime spent hunting elk in Idaho and Montana. A superb read, many color photographs and illustrations. 216 pages, hardcover only.*

Elk Hunting in the Northern Rockies, By Ed Wolff. *Uses expertise of five recognized elk hunting experts to show the five basic concepts used to hunt elk. Another of our very popular books, 162 pages, many photographs.*

So You Really Want To Be a Guide, By Dan Cherry. *The latest and single most authoritative source on what it takes to be a guide today. This book is an excellent guideline to a successful guiding career. Softcover edition only.*

Hunting Open Country Mule Deer, By Dwight Schuh. *Simply the best and most detailed book ever done for getting in close to big mule deer. The ultimate mule deer book by a recognized master, 14 chapters, 180 pages.*

Radical Elk Hunting Strategies, By Mike Lapinski. *Takes over where other books on early-season elk hunting leave off to give advice on what the hunter must do to adapt to changing conditions. 162 pages, 70 photographs.*

Cookbooks

Camp Cookbook, Featuring Recipes for Fixing Both at Home and in Camp, With Field Stories by Dale A. Burk, 216 pages, comb binding.

That Perfect Batch: The Hows and Whys of Making Sausage and Jerky, By Clem Stechelin. *Detailed instruction on techniques of making sausage and jerky at home from wild game, beef, etc. 116 pages, many photographs, comb binding.*

Cooking on Location, By Cheri Eby. *Exhaustive content for cooking on location in the outdoors, from menu planning to camp organization, meal preparation, and recipes for all sorts and styles of dishes. 139 pages, color photos and illustrations, comb binding.*

Venison As You Like It, By Ned Dobson. *A manual on getting the most from game meat, with over 200 recipes and instructions on using a variety of cooking methods. Detailed index, softcover.*

STONEYDALE PRESS PUBLISHING COMPANY
523 Main Street • Box 188
Stevensville, Montana 59870
Phone: 406-777-2729
Website: www.stoneydale.com